AFTON PRESS is delighted to bring this timely and important new book to print. When Cass Gilbert's new Minnesota Capitol opened in 1905, it was the pride of St. Paul and the envy of the nation. For one hundred years, it has been the busy hub of state government and an enduring symbol for an ever-changing Minnesota.

MINNESOTA'S CAPITOL: A Centennial Story explores and celebrates the leading role that this gleaming marble statehouse on the hill plays in our history and culture.

W. Duncan MacMillan
PRESIDENT

Teams of horses haul a massive column of marble for the new State Capitol through downtown St. Paul on East Fourth Street, between Minnesota and Robert Streets, ca. 1899.

Minnesota's Capitol

View of St. Paul (Wabasha Streetscape) by Nicholas Richard Brewer, ca. 1908.

Minnesota's Capitol

A Centennial Story

Leigh Roethke

FOREWORD BY GOVERNOR TIM PAWLENTY

INTRODUCTION BY KARAL ANN MARLING

Afton Historical Society Press

The publication of

MINNESOTA'S CAPITOL
A CENTENNIAL STORY

*and its distribution to Minnesota
schools has been made possible
by major gifts from*

Target
The Cargill Foundation

*With additional
generous gifts from*

Harlan Boss Foundation
for the Arts

Mary A. Anderson in memory
of William R. Anderson, Jr.

Xcel Energy

and

AIA Minnesota: A Society of The
American Institute of Architects

Bailey Nurseries, Inc.

Cass Gilbert Society

Ecolab

Home Federal Savings Bank

Hubbard Broadcasting Foundation

Ridgeway International, Inc.

The Whitney Foundation

Norlin and Carole Boyum

Howard and Betsy Guthmann

Malcolm McDonald

Dick and Nancy Nicholson

Front cover: Cass Gilbert's winning competition entry for the Minnesota State Capitol, 1896. Digitally colorized by Mary Susan Oleson.

Copyedited by Michele Hodgson
Designed by Mary Susan Oleson
Production assistance by Beth Williams
Printed by Pettit Network, Inc., Afton, Minnesota

Library of Congress Cataloging-in-Publication Data

Roethke, Leigh.
Minnesota's Capitol : a centennial story / by Leigh Roethke.—1st ed.
   p. cm.
ISBN 1-890434-67-1 (alk. paper)—
1. Minnesota State Capitol (Saint Paul, Minn. : 1905–)—History.
2. Saint Paul (Minn.)—Buildings, structures, etc.
I. Title.

F614.S4R64 2005
977.6'581—dc22

Printed in China   2004028157

*Afton Press receives major support
for its publishing program
from the Sarah Stevens MacMillan Foundation
and the W. Duncan MacMillan family.*

W. Duncan MacMillan   Patricia Condon Johnston
President   *Publisher*

AFTON HISTORICAL SOCIETY PRESS
P. O. Box 100, Afton, MN 55001
800-436-8443
aftonpress@aftonpress.com
www.aftonpress.com

Contents

Foreword

British statesman Winston Churchill once wrote, "We shape our buildings and thereafter, they shape us." The book you're holding is a wonderful account of the people, ideas, and materials that produced Minnesota's Capitol, and the continuing influence of this magnificent building on the life of our state.

The State Capitol is a busy place, filled with talented people who energetically try to do their best for Minnesota. Strong opinions and disagreements are voiced here, but our belief in democracy tells us that what emerges at the end of the process is probably what serves the people best.

All three branches of Minnesota's government—legislative, judicial, executive—are here under one roof, which tells me we were meant to work together to complete the people's business. This place where it all comes together—democracy's workshop—is an awesome place.

Tim Pawlenty became Minnesota's thirty-ninth governor on January 6, 2003.

One value of art and architecture is that they outlive the people who create them. Our Capitol is a lasting message to us from previous generations about what is important about our state and our people. The building is silent, but it is eloquent.

Heroes of historic battles are memorialized throughout the building to remind us that freedom isn't free, and that we should be grateful for what's been sacrificed for us. Throughout the Capitol there are countless reminders of the natural beauty and

8

Minnesota's Capitol is democracy's workshop, a place where the governor, legislators, and judges work together to represent and serve the people.

richness of Minnesota, so that even in a large indoor space, we are reminded of the wild, open spaces we love.

If you took an entire year to study every nook and cranny of this building, you'd still be left with a thousand things to learn about and try to understand. It's a bottomless treasure chest of curiosities. Although it's been my privilege to serve here for more than ten years, I've barely begun to know the Capitol. This book will help me look with a sharper eye and listen with a more open ear to the messages from Minnesota's past.

American architect Frank Lloyd Wright once wrote, "Maybe we can show government how to operate better as a result of better architecture." The beauty, innovation, and design of our Capitol does just that, bringing out the best in all who are blessed to represent the people of Minnesota.

Enjoy this history of our Capitol, and then visit and enjoy this great building, which speaks and belongs to us all.

Tim Pawlenty
GOVERNOR OF MINNESOTA

Acknowledgments

I wish to thank Afton Historical Society Press for giving me the opportunity to explore our state's beloved architectural icon, the Capitol, and to tell its story for Minnesota's young citizens. I hope this book will spark new interests in youthful readers and remind adults of just how remarkable our monument on the hill is. Special thanks go to Chuck Johnston, Patricia Johnston, Beth Williams, and all others at Afton Press for their individual contributions and tireless promotion of the project. Michele Hodgson turned her copyediting talent to the manuscript and Mary Sue Oleson designed the beautiful pages.

To Governor Tim Pawlenty, I am grateful for endorsing this book by writing the foreword. The collections of the Minnesota Historical Society were wonderful resources for me, and I am thankful to Patty Dean and Eric Mortenson for assisting with the documentation of images and objects. Tom Blanck receives my sincere appreciation for sharing his Capitol photographs. I also send my thanks to those who contributed probably without even knowing it: the Capitol tour guides for taking me through the building and up to the quadriga on numerous occasions during the earliest stages of this project.

At every point of the research and writing process, Dr. Karal Ann Marling gave me steady encouragement and kind words, and shared her extensive knowledge on all subjects Minnesotan and otherwise. Over the past six years she has been my professor, dissertation adviser, mentor, and friend. I am honored that she has contributed the introduction to this book and that she had the faith in me to suggest to Afton Press that I was ready to take on this project.

To my parents—born and/or raised in "Nordeast" Minneapolis—I send my appreciation for instilling in me that can-do Minnesota spirit. And last, but in no way least, to Jorge Zegarra, photographer extraordinaire, I send buckets of gratitude and love for his patience and eagerness to help. He visited the Capitol on many occasions and at all hours of the day to capture just the right moment when the sun shone through the skylights to illuminate the murals evenly and when the shadows fell off the outdoor statuary at the most appealing angles. His unfailing artistic eye has brought color and beauty to the pages of this book. Just as Minnesota's Capitol was the accomplishment of many Minnesotans, so too was this book. Thank you all.

The People's House

One of the best things about the Minnesota State Capitol building is its kindly hospitality to just about anybody. When the St. Paul Winter Carnival used to set up its giant sled run on the steep front lawn, the Capitol was a great place to warm up the kids between death-defying swoops down the hill. And what if it poured rain during one of the many summertime festivals held there on the grass? The Capitol offered luxurious shelter in a forest of marble columns with gilded tops.

When friends come to town, it's a tourist attraction: Can you find the gophers (for the Gopher State, of course) scurrying about the second-floor ironwork? Concert singers sound wonderful as their voices resound within the marble walls. And when concerned citizens want to make a noisy case for stiffer laws against domestic violence or increased funding for the state's colleges, the echoing vault of the Capitol rotunda is just the right spot for it. I was there just last November to pay quiet homage to the late Governor Elmer L. Andersen, who lay in state in that welcoming and sometimes contested space, the marble floor inlaid with the eight-pointed symbol of *L'Etoile du Nord.* The Star of the North. Minnesota. Our Minnesota. Our home.

In 2005, Minnesota's Capitol celebrates its one-hundredth birthday. I hope there will be noise—and plenty of souvenirs! One of the ways in which modern society has honored milestones of some importance is through celebratory excesses and keepsakes. Back in 1985, when the Capitol turned eighty, officials marked the occasion by producing a gigantic white cake that looked just like the building, right down to the last carved eagle, replicated in white frosting. Let there be even bigger cakes in 2005! And picture postcards and postage stamps. Little desktop-size replicas. Capitols imprinted on ties and scarves. On pens. On paper napkins and drinking glasses. Let there be candy Capitols, tribute songs, skits, paper hats shaped like domes. This is *our* house, Minnesota. Let's whoop it up and celebrate!

Essentially, that's what Minnesota did in the 1890s, when it determined to build the most beautiful and meaningful structure that anyone could imagine on a hill towering high above downtown St. Paul. The architect was a hometown boy who grew up on the streets below and he did Minnesota proud, with a building fashioned in the latest and most impressive of styles—what was called beaux arts classicism. In 1893, the Minnesota State Fair canceled itself for the first time in hopes that Minnesotans would visit the mighty World's Columbian Exposition being held that summer in Chicago. Designed by the greatest American architects of the day, the fair was a beaux arts vision in white ersatz marble and ornate domes. It was splendid, dignified, reminiscent of the glories of the ancient world (or the U.S. Capitol in Washington, D.C.), and startling to the eyes of visitors accustomed to the two- or three-story brick-and-stone dullness of urban America in the 1890s. The Columbian Exposition spawned what was called the "City Beautiful Movement," and Minnesota, thanks to its sumptuous plans for a new Capitol building, was making a bid to be the most beautiful spot in the land.

In *Minnesota's Capitol: A Centennial Story,* Leigh Roethke recaptures the buoyant excitement of that era and the high hopes and confidence of the Minnesotans who helped to build their shining symbol upon the hill. The luxury of imported marble and gilded statuary expressed their belief that Minnesota was marching along with the new century, down the road of progress and prosperity. The gophers, the stars, the lady's slippers, the splendid murals with titles like *Minnesota—Granary of the World* all proclaimed that the thirty-secondth state stood at the top of the list in ambition, enterprise, good taste, and sheer potential. Among these virtues, good taste was of special importance to those who chose the famous artists to paint the dreams of Minnesotans on the walls of the building. Keen to prove that they were nobody's

country cousins, they picked only the best. Today, their penchant for unclothed figures and unfamiliar subject matter makes the pictures hard to understand. We see them as lovely, colorful decoration, but we have lost a sense of the urgent meaning once attached to such scenes. In 1905, they stood for "culture" and for the notion that Minnesotans, like the ancient farmers and thinkers and trailblazers of human history, were a noble and worthy people.

For most visitors to Minnesota's State Capitol building, the most impressive feature of the exterior is the gleaming golden chariot (with horses) perched above the front door, just below the dome. This ceremonial chariot of the gods, steered forward by "Minnesota" and guided by "Agriculture" and "Industry," was the work of sculptor Daniel Chester French, the man who would later create the haunting likeness of Abraham Lincoln that occupies the great Lincoln Memorial in Washington. The Minnesota grouping, for the Capitol's façade was closely modeled after another of French's chariots, this one for the Columbian Exposition. As Leigh Roethke suggests, the reference to that earlier, well-known work made the Minnesota version instantly famous and added to the symbolic assertion that the state of Minnesota was a force to be reckoned with on the national scene. The chariot is still an object of real affection, sorely missed when it came down a few years ago for cleaning and regilding, greeted like an old friend when it returned. The golden statue is almost as important a part of the fabric of life in Minnesota as snow (or Golden Gophers).

N7 Minnesota State Capitol,
St. Paul, Minn.

This 1910-era postcard is one of legions that have celebrated Minnesota's State Capitol over the years.

The Capitol is a living, breathing repository of our collective history. Generations still unborn may pause and wonder aloud why Rudy Perpich was the only one of Minnesota's governors to pose for his official portrait with his wife. The story is an instructive one, a testimony to partnership and love, and an important reminder of the ways in which the women's movement has changed state history. Future viewers may marvel at changing standards of formality—and institutional loyalties—when they see Governor Arne Carlson decked out in his University of Minnesota regalia. Or Governor Jesse Ventura taking up the pose of *The Thinker*, once used in his playful campaign ads on television. Commenting on the official portraits of the governors amounts to a state sport. This is, after all,

our house, and we care about the relatives' pictures on display!

I hope you put down this book with a renewed feeling of affection for "the people's house" and all who dwell there—for the folks who crane their necks at the ceilings during tours, who pretend to be legislators when the seats are empty, who protest or attest in the halls, who scrutinize the governors' portraits with partisan eyes, and who stand under the gilded chariot during a sudden shower, grateful for shelter from the storm.

Karal Ann Marling
PROFESSOR, ART HISTORY
AND AMERICAN STUDIES
UNIVERSITY OF MINNESOTA

Minnesota Capitol commissioner Channing Seabury breaks ground for the new statehouse in 1896. The man (in white beard) and woman directly behind Seabury are St. Paul pioneers Auguste and Mary Larpenteur, who had been homesteaders on this land.

chapter one

Making a Monument

WITH MUCH LAUGHTER and applause, the citizens who gathered atop Wabasha Hill in St. Paul on May 6, 1896, pitched shovelfuls of earth into the horse-drawn cart that stood nearby under the care of Gust Swanson.

Channing Seabury, the steward of the project, was the first to throw off his coat, roll up his sleeves, and grab a brand new spade for a crack at the chosen ground for Minnesota's new State Capitol building. He then invited the others in attendance to take their turns with the shovel. With a bit of playful elbowing, men and women stepped up to the task. Mary and Auguste Louis Larpenteur of St. Paul each had a go at the excavating. In 1847 they had been homesteaders with a claim to the land into which they were now digging. Auguste prided himself on having driven the first stake when St. Paul was surveyed. The people at the groundbreaking were promised similar memories in years to come. They and their children would one day gaze upon the new Capitol that was to rise over downtown St. Paul.

In the flowery language of the day, one local newspaper called the groundbreaking ceremony "the first modest act in a work that shall see lifted on high a grand new Capitol, expressing the strength, the prosperity, the patriotism and the generosity of the grand commonwealth of Minnesota." The groundbreaking may have been a modest celebration, without a band or inspirational speeches, but it stirred anticipation around Minnesota. A grand new Capitol was something to look forward to. It would assert the sovereignty of the young state and boast of its successful progress from frontier territory to permanent and prosperous civilization.

FROM TERRITORY TO STATE

The United States acquired claims to lands west of the Mississippi River from France in the Louisiana Purchase of 1803. The primary native inhabitants at that time were the Dakota (Sioux), who occupied portions of present-day Wisconsin, the Dakotas, and Minnesota. Once part of the Wisconsin Territory, Minnesota was left without a government when Wisconsin became a state in 1848. A petition for territorial status for Minnesota was drafted, and Henry H. Sibley, who later became the first governor of Minnesota after statehood, presented the document to Congress. In response to the report, on March 3, 1849, the United States

**Francis Davis Millet's six-by-ten-foot painting of *The Signing of the Treaty of Traverse des Sioux,*
which commemorates the key founding event in the history of Minnesota, hangs in the Governor's
Reception Room.**

designated the land east of the Missouri and
White Earth Rivers and west of the St. Croix
and Mississippi Rivers the "Minnesota
Territory." The nonnative population in the
territory numbered around five thousand. The
federal government believed that additional
land was needed for the ongoing migration of
white settlers from the East Coast to the
Mississippi and farther west. The Ojibwa
(Chippewa) thus relinquished lands to the
north, and with the signing of the treaties at
Traverse des Sioux and Mendota in 1851, the
Dakota ceded twenty-eight million acres of
tribal lands in southwestern Minnesota, opening the door to widespread settlement.

American enterprise and frontier spirit paid off.
The new Minnesota Territory saw a brisk
upturn in settlement. During the nineteenth
century, pushing west, settling the land, and
building civilization—despite the displacement
of native peoples—was believed to be the ful-
fillment of what Americans called manifest des-
tiny. Politicians and orators spread the belief
that Americans were fated to move westward,
toward the Pacific, "civilizing" as they went.
For new European immigrants and easterners
searching for better lives, the land west of the
Mississippi seemed to offer limitless opportunities. Frontier life was a challenge, but it also
held the promise of freedom and prosperity.

Seizing quickly upon the opportunity, boosters and land speculators jumped into action to promote the Minnesota Territory and its resources for their own profit. Minnesota was dogged at midcentury by the perception that it was the "American Siberia," meaning that, like Russia's Siberia, it was bitterly cold and isolated from established metropolitan centers. But in 1854 a railroad line linking Chicago with Rock Island, Illinois, was completed. Travelers could get off the train at Rock Island and then board a steamboat that would take them up the Mississippi to St. Paul. The entire trip from Chicago took a mere thirty hours. Minnesota was now only four days from New York! That same year, railroad contractors sponsored the Grand Excursion to promote the Upper Mississippi region. Traveling from Rock Island, hundreds of people joined ex-president Millard Fillmore on a voyage up the river by steamboat to St. Paul. Minnesota was remote wilderness no longer.

Boosters printed and dispersed guides that extolled Minnesota's clear waters, vast forests, fertile land, and endless business opportunities. One particularly enthusiastic promoter,

Minnesota's first Capitol (circled) overlooks the fledgling community of St. Paul in 1855, as painted by S. Andrew Holmes.

Minnesota's Capitol

James Madison Goodhue, founder of the *Minnesota Pioneer,* ran ads and columns in his newspaper bragging and boasting about the bounties of the northland. These campaigns proved successful: steamboats brought thousands of men, women, and their families to put down roots and try their luck in agriculture or business in Minnesota. By 1857 the population of the Minnesota Territory had swelled to one hundred and fifty thousand inhabitants. In May 1862, Congress passed the Homestead Act, which granted any homesteader up to 160 acres of unoccupied federal land provided that the settler lived on it, built a shelter, and farmed it for five years. Or the head of a family could purchase the land for $1.25 an acre after six months. Newcomers relocated from New England, New York, and the Great Lakes states. A great many were recent immigrants from Ireland, Germany, Scandinavia, and other European countries.

The capital of the Minnesota Territory was St. Paul. The first meeting of the Territorial

Artist Joseph Rusling Meeker's *Minnesota Harvest Field* depicts rural Minnesota in 1877.

The first Territorial Legislature met in the Central House, a St. Paul hotel and boarding house.

Legislature convened in the dining room of the Central House, a St. Paul hotel and boarding house kept by "old daddy Burton" and his wife on Second and Minnesota Streets. In 1853 a new Territorial Capitol was constructed at Tenth and Cedar Streets. Because Minnesota's new territorial governor and legislators were immigrants themselves, it was not surprising that their first Capitol resembled civic architecture seen in the older eastern states. It was a symmetrical brick building with a small dome over the center. At the entrance, columns reached up two full stories, topped with a triangular form called a pediment, which gave the building the dignified look of an ancient Greek temple. When Minnesota became the thirty-second state to enter the Union on May 11, 1858, the building on Tenth and Cedar officially became the state's first Capitol. It was twice remodeled during the 1870s to add more space and to suit changing tastes in design, but in 1881 the building burned down.

By 1883 St. Paul architect Leroy Buffington had completed Minnesota's second State Capitol on the same site. It was a four-story building made of pressed red brick from Red Wing, Minnesota. A tall tower rose from its center, as if to call attention to the building. Yet from the beginning, the beauty of its elaborate interior woodwork and the spaciousness of its chambers did not prevent complaints of overcrowding and air "utterly unfit for human beings to breathe." Within a decade, plans for a new Capitol building were already in the works.

THE CAPITOL COMPETITION

During the 1893 legislative session, an expenditure of two million dollars was approved for the construction of a new statehouse in St. Paul. In view of the economic depression of 1893, this was a moderate sum for the time. Beyond the shortcomings of Buffington's "lemon," as it had been dubbed, the legislators had good reason to call for a new Capitol

The Van Dusen Grain Elevator, by Alexis Jean Fournier, shows a vibrant, industrial Minneapolis.

building. Minnesota had successfully shaken off its "American Siberia" reputation.

Immigration and industry had boomed during the twenty years between 1870 and 1890. In 1893 one and a half million people lived in Minnesota. Minneapolis and St. Paul had grown into important centers for flour milling, sawmilling, and transportation. With their flourishing businesses, entertainments, and society life, the Twin Cities had become quite

Indeed, a new capitol was needed to showcase the attainment of the young state, to honor its past, and to reflect the optimism and pride instilled by half a century of steady growth. Minnesota was not alone in this sentiment. The years following the Civil War had seen a boom in state capitol building across the country. Older states were outgrowing their capitols, and the more lavish tastes of the era called for grander architectural expressions. With wars of the nineteenth century still fresh in citizens' memories,

Minnesota's first official State Capitol was built of red brick at Tenth and Cedar Streets in 1853.

cosmopolitan. At huge international fairs in Paris and Barcelona, and at the 1893 World's Columbian Exposition in Chicago, Minnesota was well represented as a leading producer of wheat, flour, lumber, iron ore, and dairy products. One guidebook to the fair described Minnesota as "the young giantess of the upper Mississippi, in all her youthful vigor, proud of the past and hopeful of the future."

new capitol buildings could house shrines to a state's fallen heroes. And like Minnesota, other newer western states wanted buildings to symbolize their prosperity and permanence.

Between the close of the Civil War and 1890, new capitols were built in thirteen states. Rivalry was involved: each state wanted to outdo the rest. The buildings were some of the

In 1883 Minnesota's second Capitol went up atop the ashes of the first Capitol.

most expensive architectural projects of the nineteenth century. Projected budgets often were exceeded to upgrade materials or designs to make for more impressive grandeur. Iowa, Minnesota's neighbor to the south, launched its capitol project in 1870; Wisconsin followed Minnesota after a fire damaged its old capitol building in 1904; and South Dakota broke ground for its new capitol in 1905.

The business of capitol building was already well established by 1893. Minnesota had enough examples elsewhere to know the process and its pitfalls. With the funding for a new statehouse approved, Governor Knute Nelson appointed a State Capitol board of commissioners to oversee the project, the standard course taken by other states. The seven members came from varied walks of life. Some were Republicans and some were Democrats. Each delegate represented a congressional district. By the end of the project, four more men had been added to the group. The original seven all hailed from the East, but had made Minnesota their home. Channing Seabury, a successful wholesale grocer from St. Paul, was appointed vice president of the board. In practice, he was given the lion's share of responsibility for overseeing the creation of the Minnesota State Capitol.

The first order of business was the selection of a building site. The board of commissioners chose a large plot bordered by University Avenue, Cedar Street, Park Avenue, Wabasha Street, and Central Avenue. The choice of a piece of land adjoining University Avenue was a diplomatic one. University was the main thoroughfare between the Twin Cities. Further, the location on a hill above the Mississippi would command authority for the building that would symbolize the sovereign state.

With the real estate secured, the board of commissioners needed an architect and a design. They would find their architect through a nationwide competition—or, in the end, *two* competitions. Because of the visibility of the buildings and the money involved, state capitol commissions were highly sought after by architects, who entered competitions all around the country. Minnesota's first competition was advertised in Chicago, Boston, and Minnesota cities in June 1894. It was open to any qualified architect, and the board received fifty-six entries. Each architect submitted a drawing and a written proposal. Disappointingly, the competition's architectural advisers, Edmund M. Wheelright of Boston and Henry Ives Cobb of Chicago, decided that all the designs were awful. What is more, of the fifty-six entrants, only eleven were Minnesotans.

Certain competition rules had been cause for alarm among members of the Minnesota chapter of the American Institute of Architects, a professional association that voiced its reservations through prominent St. Paul architect

Cass Gilbert. Money and authority were the major issues. In a private meeting with Channing Seabury, Gilbert had asked if the winning architect could also serve as the project supervisor and if the stipend for the winner could be increased. But the board had approved neither request, and the design contest had gone ahead as planned amid rumors that respectable architects would boycott the contest.

Gilbert saw himself and his colleagues as professional architects, "artists" who were entitled to respect and professional fees. This was a new concept in the United States, especially outside the major eastern cities, and Minnesota's board of commissioners was slow to respond. Talented amateurs, without formal education in architecture, had designed most buildings in America up to that time. The professional architect was a new breed who came at a new price. A man of conviction, Gilbert brought the reservations of the American Institute of Architects back to the board. Giving the chosen architect a supervisory role would ensure his creative control over the project, he argued. The increased fee for the winning architect would attract higher-quality entries from esteemed professionals. In the end, the artist triumphed.

Gilbert's persistence, compounded by the weakness of the initial batch of designs, was enough to scrap the first competition. For the second go-around, only selected architects were invited to submit entries. This, the board anticipated, would result in stronger designs. Cass Gilbert was now a contender, and the forty-one designs received were soon whittled down to five promising finalists: Wendell and Humphreys of Denver; George R. Mann of St. Louis; Bassford, Traphagen, and Fitzpatrick of St. Paul and Duluth; Clarence H. Johnston of St. Paul; and Cass Gilbert of St. Paul.

In October 1895, the State Capitol board of commissioners awarded the project to Gilbert. But the award was not without controversy. When voting by ballot had produced no consensus, Seabury had taken the matter into his own hands. He moved that Gilbert be named the winner by voice vote, a motion that was seconded and adopted by the committee. Was

there something fishy about the selection process? At least one of the other competing architects and one reporter from the *Minneapolis Journal* thought so. They complained that Gilbert was a friend of Seabury, which gave the architect an unfair edge. But the general response to Gilbert's selection was favorable. He was, after all, a western architect, which earned him the approval of the sons and daughters of proud pioneers. And he was a St. Paul man too. Besides, there was no time to quibble. There was work to be done. By the following spring, ground was broken on Wabasha Hill. On May 6, 1896, the great project began.

The Minnesota State Capitol board of commissioners: Edgar Weaver, John De Laittre, C. H. Graves, Channing Seabury, George A. Du Toit, H. W. Lamberton, and E. E. Corliss.

How St. Paul Got (and Kept) the Capitol

Wrangling over a governmental center is a classic American story. The location for the U.S. Capitol was a point of contention after the Revolutionary War. States argued over the Capitol until President George Washington chose a plot of land along the Potomac River. America's state capitols often have similar stories.

When the Wisconsin Territory was established in 1836, for example, it sparked a long struggle over where to locate the seat of its government. When Congress established the Minnesota Territory in 1849, it authorized the Territorial Legislature to choose a city for a temporary capital. They chose St. Paul. What followed, however, was a comic drama. Full of schemes and follies, it was perpetrated by rough-hewn frontiersmen driven by their own wildly different interests.

Located about halfway between the Minnesota Territory's northern and southern boundaries,

The log chapel that begot St. Paul.

the city of St. Paul was a reasonable choice. It had become a strategic outpost for the U.S. Army when Fort Snelling was built in 1819. After 1841, a settlement grew up around a small log church built by Father Lucien Galtier and dedicated to St. Paul; the church gave the town its name. Eight years later St. Paul was a booming Mississippi River town.

St. Paul was by no means the *only* city in Minnesota, however. Though efforts were made to distribute important symbolic resources fairly—Stillwater got the prison and St. Anthony got the University of Minnesota—imminent statehood made various groups rethink the capital issue.

In 1855 the St. Peter Land Company was established and its proprietors set out to grow their property into a boomtown. With would-be profits dancing in their heads, they hatched a plan to have the capital removed from St. Paul to St. Peter. Certain territorial legislators and officers,

"Jolly Joe" Rolette, who kept Minnesota's capital in St. Paul, poses in frontiersman duds.

it seems, were also in a position to profit from the scheme.

Without much fuss, the Territorial Legislature passed a bill to remove the capital. The St. Peter Land Company had offered $20,000 for a capitol building and the land on which to build it, and the legislature took them up on it. But before the governor could sign the bill, it had to be enrolled (that is, a final copy needed to be made). The bill landed on the desk of a legislator named Joe Rolette, chair of the Enrollment Committee. Legend has it that "Jolly Joe," a St. Paul loyalist, made off with the document and holed up in a hotel attic, where he bided his time playing poker with unnamed co-conspirators.

When the matter was called up for final passage on February 28, 1857, Rolette and the bill were nowhere to be found. Without the bill and Jolly Joe, the other legislators found themselves in a pickle. Their own rules held that they could not commence business until all members were present. What's more, they had to remain in the Council Chamber until everyone was accounted for. The desperate legislators sent a man to search for Rolette, but that man (according to one version of the story) joined the poker game and didn't return.

Four days went by. Food and pillows were brought into the chamber, where the lawmakers now dwelled. After 123 hours, they suspended their meeting on March 5, but returned the next day to try again. Still no

Jolly Joe! At the stroke of midnight on March 7, the council president announced that the time allowed by law for a legislative session had run out and adjourned the body.

Wily Joe Rolette, the man who saved the capital, became a hero in St. Paul. But in another twist of history, while all this was going on, another copy of the bill had made its way to the desk of territorial governor Willis Gorman, who signed it into law. Believing in the legality of the bill, the St. Peter Land Company went ahead and erected a capitol building. The Territorial Legislature never met in that building. And in 1858, when Minnesota gained statehood, the Territorial Capitol at Tenth and Cedar Streets in St. Paul, where this drama had played out, became Minnesota's first State Capitol building.

Between 1858 and 1893, further unsuccessful efforts were made to snatch the capital from St. Paul, including five attempts to move it to Kandiyohi and one to Minneapolis. When the first Capitol burned down in 1881, the ashes had not yet cooled when the St. Peter Land Company was talking about another capital removal. Governor John S. Pillsbury would hear nothing of it; he quickly made an appropriation for a second Capitol building in St. Paul. Pillsbury's action was a temporary, delaying measure. Not until 1893, when the Minnesota Legislature voted to build the new Capitol in St. Paul, did its members bring an end to forty-four years of statehouse tug-of-war. Thus opened a new chapter in Minnesota history.

LAYING THE CORNER STONE OF THE MINNESOTA STATE CAPITOL JULY 27TH 1898   HAAS BROS

It was a grand day for all who came to the site of the new State Capitol to celebrate the laying of the cornerstone, which is seen here suspended from the cable of an unseen crane.

chapter two

Minnesota—and Proud of It!

ON JULY 27, 1898, a nice warm day, crowds once again gathered atop Wabasha Hill. They had come to watch the laying of the cornerstone of Minnesota's new Capitol.

There was more hoopla and pageantry than at the groundbreaking. Notable citizens delivered speeches about Minnesota's strength, its progress since the pioneer days, and the Capitol that would soon become the pride of their state. Mounted police led a parade of marching bands, soldiers, veterans, and the fire brigade to the building site. Foundations for the new Capitol had been laid and the subbasement was almost finished.

A reviewing stand built especially for the day spilled over with people watching through the windows of the half-built basement. Some dangled their feet over the walls for the best view of the ceremony going on below amid the sea of men and women wearing light summer hats. The granite cornerstone hung from a derrick by cables decorated with red, white, and blue streamers. American flags fluttered in the pleasant breeze. Eighty-three-year-old Alexander Ramsey, the first territorial governor and second state governor of Minnesota, laid the mortar for the cornerstone with a ceremonial silver trowel. The trowel's handle was made from wood taken from the Central House, where Ramsey and the first Territorial Legislature had assembled in 1849.

Governor Alexander Ramsey used a silver trowel to help lay the Capitol's cornerstone.

29

SOMETHING OLD, SOMETHING NEW

The crowds at the cornerstone ceremony were excited about their new Capitol. They had been hearing about it for three years, and seeing progress on the hill for themselves had people agog. Newspapers asserted that the building was going to be grander than anything most Minnesotans had ever seen—a true wonder. This meant a great deal for people only a few years removed from the frontier. If the Capitol project was evidence, Minnesota still had plenty of the old can-do frontier spirit.

The building was going to be big and expensive. Cass Gilbert had won the Capitol commission with his design for a three-story stone structure. There would be three chambers radiating from an open central space (called a rotunda) that would be crowned with an imposing dome. There would be columns and sculptures and lots of marble.

Gilbert's design indeed looked like it might be more at home in an ancient European city than St. Paul. But that was part of the scheme. The State Capitol board of commissioners wanted a building that would announce to the rest of the country that their state was no longer a wilderness outpost; it had grown into a modern, civilized society. A fancy, European-

This postcard depicts an 1898 drawing of the Capitol by Cass Gilbert. In the early stages of the project, the architect had envisioned more sculptures on the roof and a slightly different portico, or front porch.

looking building would claim for Minnesota the culture and sophistication of the Old World. The Capitol would be a point of pride for the youthful state.

Gilbert's design borrowed elements from the architecture of ancient Greece and Rome as well as from the Renaissance period in Italy and France. American architecture had a long history of borrowing and adapting. Because the colonial United States was a place of log cabins and modest houses, American architects took many of their ideas for public buildings from those in Europe. But they did not just copy old buildings. There are no buildings in Europe that look exactly like the Minnesota State Capitol.

In 1898 there were no buildings in Minnesota that looked like Gilbert's design, either. The style had recently made its way west from France, via the East Coast. Despite looking old, Minnesota's Capitol would actually be up-to-date. Men with machines would build it of stone, iron, and steel. It would have electricity, elevators, telephones, steam heat, fireproofing, and indoor toilets on two floors. (How better to signify the end of frontier life?) But on the surface it would have the look of the sixteenth-century Italian Renaissance, the age of Michelangelo and the domed Cathedral of St. Peter's.

Cass Gilbert borrowed from the past to say something about the present. For many people during the nineteenth century, marble buildings with domes and columns stood for the admirable ideas of the cultures that built them. Borrowing the look of those buildings showed that Americans also aspired to those ideals.

AMERICAN CLASSICS

After the Revolutionary War, the American republic needed new symbols to represent its government and its goals. Architecture, as the most visible of public symbols, was particularly important. But rather than creating entirely new forms, builders emulated the architecture of the ancient world. Ancient Greece was believed to be the birthplace of civilized western culture and democracy, and Rome's republican form of government was used as the basis for America's. Buildings that borrowed Greco-Roman elements, it was thought, would best represent the virtue and order to which the American republic aspired.

The architects who built new statehouses along the eastern seaboard during the early nineteenth century combined Greek and Roman elements such as columns and domes with the materials they already knew. Soon this became the norm for important civic buildings in America. Frontier builders wanted to bring the glory of the ancients to the West. Minnesota's first State Capitol building, for example, had a small dome and a columned front porch (called a portico) topped with a triangular mass (a pediment), similar to elements found in a Greek temple. Such structures stood out amid the wilderness and the hastily built wooden structures of frontier towns. They commanded respect from eastern snobs who might otherwise think that the West was unsophisticated.

President George Washington laid the cornerstone of the U.S. Capitol in September 1793.

The completion of the soaring white dome of the U.S. Capitol in Washington, D.C., during the Civil War had a sizeable effect on the evolving look of American statehouses. One speaker at the cornerstone ceremony in St. Paul remarked that Gilbert's domed building was "educated with the familiarity with the great Capitol building in Washington." The popularity and democratic meaning of the federal Capitol's dome made the building an ideal model for state capitol designers.

ALL THAT GLITTERS

During the years following the Civil War, capitol building in the United States boomed alongside industry and big business. The building campaigns of several states reflected America's surging wealth. Classicism was still the norm for civic architecture, but the more elegant and decorative Renaissance version of classical architecture came into style. The word "Renaissance" refers to the revival of classic antiquity in art, architecture, and literature in parts of Europe from the fourteenth through the sixteenth centuries. Renaissance buildings were more ornate and elegant. Renaissance columns were fancier. States replaced their aging capitols with extravagant showplaces in the Renaissance manner. The new interiors were adorned with expensive materials, carvings, and sculptures. Renowned painters decorated wall spaces in places far afield of the artistic centers of New York and Boston.

Before announcing its first design competition, Minnesota's State Capitol board of commissioners set out on a state capitol junket. What they saw in the recently completed capitols in Indiana, Illinois, Michigan, and Iowa were many tall domes, all inspired by the U.S. Capitol in Washington, D.C. Minnesota's neighbor to the south, Iowa, completed its

capitol at a cost of $2,873,294 in 1886. It boasted five domes—one over each of its four corners and a skyward-reaching central dome that was constructed of steel and stone and then gilded with twenty-three-karat gold.

Cass Gilbert kept current with new developments in design, not only in the Midwest but also back East. In New York, the leading architects were Charles F. McKim, William R. Mead, and Stanford White. Gilbert knew these men. He had worked as an assistant in their

The Iowa State Capitol in Des Moines has *five* domes, four of them visible in this 1910 postcard.

New York offices when he was starting out. On the East Coast, McKim, Mead, and White were designing buildings in a modern version of Renaissance classicism sometimes called beaux arts (French for "fine arts"). Its name comes from the leading art school in nineteenth-century Paris, the École des Beaux-Arts.

Beaux arts buildings followed strict rules of proportion and order. Beauty was to be found in absolute perfection. They were imposing structures meant to stir emotion in those who gazed upon them. Their exteriors were light-colored—shimmering and pure—and typically ornamented with elegant carved garlands, flowers, or sculpted shields called cartouches. Numerous leading American architects studied at the École des Beaux-Arts in Paris, and they brought what they learned back to the United States. By the 1880s, beaux arts classicism was the favored style for grandiose public buildings such as museums, libraries, railway stations, and government buildings in large cities along the Atlantic seaboard. But it was a midwestern city that gave the beaux arts style its national popularity.

THE COLUMBIAN EXPOSITION

The 1893 World's Columbian Exposition in Chicago, a commemoration of the four hundredth anniversary of the discovery of America by Columbus, was the last and greatest of the nineteenth century's World's Fairs. Twenty-seven million people from all over the world traveled to Chicago; Minnesota even canceled its State Fair that year to encourage folks to go! Attractions included Buffalo Bill

Cody's "Wild West Show," the first Ferris wheel, and a "Street in Cairo." But the biggest attraction of the fair itself was the "White City."

It was important for Chicago to show that the West could be just as sophisticated as older eastern cities, especially since Chicago had won the honor of hosting the fair in a heated battle with New York City. Chicago proved itself by bringing the architecture of the East to the Midwest. For the 1893 World's Columbian Exposition, Daniel Burnham of Chicago and the McKim, Mead, and White firm of New York designed a metropolis of gleaming beaux arts buildings that surrounded a lagoon featuring Renaissance-inspired fountains and sculpture. The light, bright color of these buildings earned them the nickname the "White City." It was Chicago's version of Renaissance Europe. Unfortunately, the buildings were constructed of a temporary, plaster-based mixture. But the effect while it lasted was magnificent. Visitors agreed that there was nothing like this "dream city" anywhere else in America.

The World's Columbian Exposition moved American architects to plan extensive beaux arts schemes all over the United States. They designed public buildings with expansive lawns, wide boulevards, and open park spaces to beautify cities blemished by the ugliness of industrialization. In the place of dirty, poverty-stricken urban streets they envisioned magnificent monuments recalling the splendor of Europe's great cities. They believed beauty could inspire virtue in the hearts of all people.

The Court of Honor was the splendid centerpiece of the 1893 World's Columbian Exposition.

This beaux arts–inspired "City Beautiful Movement" touched and marked Twin Cities architecture: Emmanuel Louis Masqueray, a French architect trained at the École des Beaux-Arts, designed the imposing Cathedral of St. Paul in 1905. Cass Gilbert designed the Northrop Mall in this style for the University of Minnesota in 1908. In 1914 one of his students designed the Gateway Park and Pavilion (destroyed in the 1950s) for downtown Minneapolis. And the classically proportioned Minneapolis Institute of Arts, designed by the New York firm of McKim, Mead, and White, opened in 1915.

Gilbert believed that the size, ordered proportions, and sophistication of beaux arts classicism perfectly suited the symbolic heart of Democratic Minnesota. His basic plan for the State Capitol follows the American tradition of capitol design: It is a symmetrical, domed building with a central, columned porch. Its primary dome is tall, like the dome of the federal Capitol and Michelangelo's dome for St. Peter's in Rome. Two other shallow domes cover the wings of Minnesota's Capitol building, one for the Senate Chamber and the other for the House of Representatives. The exterior is decorated with carved garlands of

A STONE BY ANY OTHER NAME

The kind of stone to be used to build the new statehouse became a much debated and thorny issue. Gilbert wanted white marble quarried in Georgia for his Capitol, if the money could be found. White marble was the traditional stone for monumental architecture in Europe and America. It is both durable and brilliant. The federal Capitol was faced with pure white marble, and Chicago's "White City" looked as though it had been built of the same stone. For Gilbert, white marble was the historically and artistically correct choice. Less expensive, locally quarried stone, such as granite or sandstone, would turn his building into a "gloomy, fortress-like pile," lacking the gleam and sparkle of marble.

Bringing white marble all the way from Georgia would be much more expensive than using Minnesota stone; exploiting native materials was one way to keep costs down. It also allowed local people to contribute to and see themselves reflected in the Capitol that was being paid for with their tax dollars. And why, Gilbert's opponents objected, should big contracts go to another state, especially a southern state that Minnesota's veterans associated with the Civil War?

The problem was that Minnesota stone is not white. Winona limestone was an option because of its light color, but it was ruled out for not being as long lasting as marble. Gilbert knew for a fact that there was no stone native to Minnesota that equaled the brilliance and strength of Georgia marble.

A worker carves one of the twelve stone eagles that surround the base of the Capitol dome.

fruit and flowers and sculptures representing the virtues of good citizenship. There are sculpted shields bearing the initial letter M for Minnesota. On the middle dome there are eagles to symbolize democracy and stars that represent the state motto *L'Etoile du Nord* (French for "the star of the North"). A gilded quadriga (a four-horse chariot) sits at the base of the dome. This is Renaissance classicism with a taste of Minnesota.

In August 1897, the stone issue erupted. Under pressure from local stonecutters, the State Capitol commissioners were leaning toward the conclusion that Minnesota's statehouse should be constructed from Minnesota stone. Gilbert lobbied hard for marble, but he saw the political handwriting on the wall. If the visible upper walls were marble, he acquiesced, then a foundation of Minnesota granite would be acceptable.

After days of heated debate, a deal was struck. The board was split on the decision, but Channing Seabury again became Gilbert's ally. In an effort to please everyone, it was agreed that the basement would be constructed of St. Cloud granite, the foundation of the dome and the exterior piers would be made of Kettle River sandstone, and the most visible upper section of the building would be built with white Georgia marble. Gilbert's compromise did not wholly please Minnesota's quarry owners and their supporters, however. One incensed fellow directed his disapproval to the Capitol commission: "Damn the traitors who did the murderous deed!"

Gaining each day in grandeur, the Capitol already looked regal in July 1903. The commissioners signed a contract for "General Construction of the New State Capitol Building" with the Butler-Ryan Company of St. Paul. While the building was under construction, however, Walter and William Butler bought out their partner Mike Ryan and changed the firm's name firm to Butler Brothers.

Minnesota-grown apples were used to re-create Fort Snelling at 1901's Pan-American Exposition.

Construction progressed rapidly after the stone hullabaloo died down and the cornerstone was in place. As the century turned, the marble walls rose. By 1900 the structure bore a close resemblance to Gilbert's drawing, but without its dome. The drum—the vertical cylinder on which the dome sits—and the low copper domes over the wings were ready by the spring of 1901. Summer saw the completion of the exterior carvings. The main dome would be next. But before the construction of the great dome even began, Gilbert's Capitol was a symbol of pride for Minnesota.

A BUTTER CAPITOL IN BUFFALO

The 1901 Pan-American Exposition in Buffalo, New York, was an international stage for states to show off the products of their creative minds and industries. With the confidence of a state on top of its game, Minnesota did just that. J. W. Underwood of the Jewell Nursery of Lake City contributed an attraction that had been popular at the Minnesota State Fair—an eighteen-foot-high rotating model of historic Fort Snelling made of ninety bushels of Minnesota-grown apples. Atop the Minnesota booth within the exposition's Agricultural Building sat "The Woman in Grain," a figure cleverly fashioned from local crops. Visitors to the Manufacturers and Liberal Arts Building couldn't miss the award-winning display of flour sacks emblazoned with the trademarks of Minnesota's mills. And every day in that same building, the Pillsbury-Washburn Milling Company handed out more than fifteen hundred fresh-baked rolls smothered with creamy Minnesota butter. Displaying food products with an artful flair was a nineteenth-century tradition that continued to delight fairgoers in Buffalo.

Of all the edible marvels at the Pan-American Exposition, however, it was a building in butter that asserted Minnesota's superiority. The attraction began as a request from the Board of Pan-American Managers for Minnesota to the State Capitol board of commissioners for a plaster model of the new statehouse to be displayed in Buffalo. Gilbert's Capitol, after all, was to be an impressive Minnesota achievement and would boast of the progress of the North Star State. But how could such a model be built in the four months left before the opening of the Buffalo fair? Unexpectedly, John Karl Daniels, "a promising sculptor" from St. Paul, offered his services. His butter sculpture of a cow and dairymaid for the Minnesota State Fair had earned Daniels some measure of esteem the previous summer.

Daniels and his friend, W. S. Jensen, proposed to build the model of the State Capitol in butter. The Crescent Creamery of St. Paul furnished more than one thousand pounds of the highest-grade butter Minnesota had to offer. Minnesota's Pan-American board secured the most prominent space in the Dairy Building, directly in front of the entrance. A butter Capitol was sure to draw people in by the sheer force of its novelty. Every day for six weeks, John K. Daniels, assisted by his brother, Hacon Daniels,

worked fifteen or more hours on the sculpture in a large refrigerated glass case made especially for their task. The finished model was five-and-a-half feet tall from the tip of its dome to the green velvet that represented the Capitol lawn. It was twelve feet wide and seven feet deep. Its newfangled electrically refrigerated case protected the dairy extravaganza from Buffalo's sweltering summer. "It would make quite a sizable playhouse for children, as to size," one witness decided, "but as the butter house that represents Minnesota's greatest industry is kept in a refrigerated room it would scarcely prove enjoyable as a playhouse."

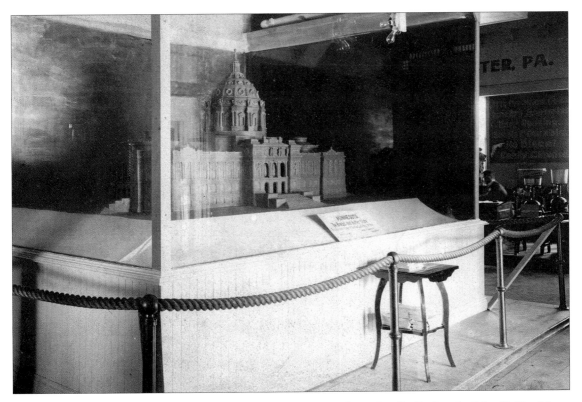

Minnesota's State Capitol was sculpted in butter by up-and-coming St. Paul artist John K. Daniels for the 1901 Pan-American Exposition.

The butter Capitol was a sensation. Governor Samuel R. Van Sant was on hand for Minnesota Day at the exposition. A butter booster, he bragged to a crowd of reporters: "Our butter takes the premium at every exposition held—at Paris, at the World's Fair, at Omaha—and it is going to take it here if they don't pack the judges against us. So great have we become known in that respect that we have changed our name from the Gopher State to the Bread and Butter State of the Union." Minnesota's Pan-American board proclaimed that "thousands of people visited the exposition who otherwise would not have gone, especially to see this model, and every one who saw it carried away with him or her the impression that Minnesota was a great and enterprising state."

Cass Gilbert, like many of his fellow architects, spoke about how grandiose buildings symbolized the stability and dignity of a state through their beauty and historical forms. But Minnesota's progress and achievements were just as well represented in that refrigerated case in Buffalo. The State Capitol in butter displayed the pride that Minnesotans felt in building such a magnificent, sophisticated monument. But it made no difference whether the state was represented in marble or in butter in 1901: Minnesotans were just plain proud to be Minnesotans.

This mammoth frosted cake celebrated the Capitol's eightieth birthday in 1985.

Architect Cass Gilbert

Cass Gilbert had a handlebar mustache and the bold character to match it. He built his architectural career out of a fierce determination to succeed. Along the way, he changed the face of St. Paul.

Born in Zanesville, Ohio, in 1859, Gilbert traveled with his family by steamboat down the Ohio River and up the Mississippi to Minnesota when he was nine. He came of age in St. Paul at a time when the city itself was growing up. After attending public school, he entered the world of architecture at age seventeen by taking a job in the offices of a small architectural firm in St. Paul.

In 1878 Gilbert went east to Cambridge, Massachusetts, where he enrolled in an architecture program at the Massachusetts Institute of Technology. He attended classes for one year, but his heart was not in academic learning. He wanted to see great architecture of the world firsthand. His wanderlust took him to Europe, a path well trodden by many young Americans of his time. Gilbert traveled throughout England, France, and Italy, sketching and painting architecturally famous

Cass Gilbert, ca. 1907, admired European design.

buildings and sites that would inspire him throughout his career.

Gilbert returned to the United States in 1880 and took a job as a draftsman in the recently established New York offices of the architects McKim, Mead, and White. There he honed his skills as an architect and developed profes-

sional connections. By January 1883, he was back in St. Paul to represent the New York firm in building projects under consideration by the Northern Pacific Railroad. The Northern Pacific work fell through, but Gilbert was not without local prospects. He joined the St. Paul architectural firm of James Knox Taylor, a college friend from MIT.

By 1885 Gilbert and Taylor were business partners and social climbers, trying to capitalize on St. Paul's rapid growth. Between 1885 and 1892 they won more than fifty commissions for churches, homes, and commercial buildings, including the Endicott Building in downtown St. Paul. In 1887 Gilbert married Julia Tappan Finch, a well-to-do society girl from Milwaukee, Wisconsin. The economic depression of the early 1890s took its toll on the Gilbert and Taylor partnership, however. Taylor left for Philadelphia, while Gilbert continued his architectural practice in St. Paul.

Gilbert's famous skyscraper, the 1910 Woolworth Building, still stands in New York City.

Gilbert was determined to be successful. In 1892 he helped found the Minnesota chapter of the American Institute of Architects and was elected its president. His design skills and dogged determination won him the Minnesota State Capitol commission in 1895. It was the project that would make his career. While construction of the Capitol was under way in St. Paul, Gilbert was looking east. He opened a second office in New York City in March 1899. From there he would work on the eighteen-story Broadway Chambers Building, his first major New York job. Winning another large New York

Gilbert (with elbow on table) and his staff display blueprints of the Capitol during its construction.

commission for the Custom House prompted him to move his family from St. Paul to New York in 1900. He designed New York's Woolworth Building in 1910, and after 1932 he oversaw the construction of his design for the U.S. Supreme Court in Washington, D.C.

Gilbert kept his St. Paul office open until 1911. Some said he had burned too many bridges with local quarry owners during the State Capitol project, making later Minnesota com-

missions hard to come by. Yet Gilbert stayed the course. Between 1906 and 1922, his projects included the master plan for Northrop Mall on the Minneapolis campus of the University of Minnesota, as well as the Soldiers' and Sailors' Monument in Duluth, the Mannheimer Fountain at St. Paul's Como Park, and the Ninth District Federal Reserve Bank in downtown Minneapolis. Cass Gilbert died in New York in 1934 at the age of seventy-five, wreathed in honors.

An awe-inspiring rotunda greets visitors upon their arrival at Minnesota's Capitol. Cass Gilbert designed the inlaid marble floor with its eight-pointed *L'Etoile du Nord* ("Star of the North") motif. The red points are Numidian (African) marble, radiating from a ring of dark blue Georgian marble. Gilbert used many beautiful marble varieties from Italy, France, and Greece to build and decorate his magnificent Capitol.

chapter three

Minnesota's Showplace

IT WAS THE COUNTLESS incandescent lights and the decorations that most impressed visitors at the Minnesota State Capitol when it was first lit for the public on January 2, 1905.

All day—until they were shepherded out at close that night—thousands of Minnesotans passed up and down the grand stairways and through the halls, admiring the elegant interior and "drinking in the beauties of the decorations." Just before noon, the huge chandelier was hoisted into place two hundred feet above the center of the rotunda. The eight-foot sphere made of thousands of light bulbs and reflective crystals was illuminated for the first time that evening.

There were still a few details to be attended to before the interior would be finished. The Capitol project was rushed to meet its January 1905 deadline, and the scaffolding was removed from the hallways only a few hours before visitors arrived. The mural decorations were nearly all in place, except for those in the Supreme

Modern electric light standards illuminated the new Capitol.

Court Chamber and one or two paintings elsewhere. And there was quite a bit of work yet to be done in the Governor's Reception Room, where men still stood on scaffolding to finish the decorative painting on the walls and ceilings. Nonetheless, the public marveled at how complete the Capitol appeared. Minnesota's citizens had been following its construction since the groundbreaking nine years before, and now, after nearly a decade and an expenditure of four and a half million dollars, the Capitol was ready for business.

Even before the building was completed, Minnesota's Capitol was known everywhere. The butter model at the 1901 Pan-American Exposition in Buffalo, New York, alerted non-Minnesotans to the grand building rising in St. Paul. Architecture magazines published Cass Gilbert's design, and photographers zealously documented its construction. But the Capitol was launched into stardom when it officially opened in 1905. It was a place of government. It was also a popular attraction for locals and visitors alike.

Minnesota's Capitol

Once picture postcards were introduced to the public at the 1893 World's Columbian Exposition, they became a popular form of communication. The penny postcard industry had a slew of photographers and illustrators creating images of famous sites and events. souvenirs. Tourists to the Twin Cities took home souvenirs adorned with images of Fort Snelling, Minnehaha Falls, or Como Park. And the grand new Capitol that was built to impress did just that. Capitols large and small, two- and three-dimensional, became popular

The nearly completed Minnesota Capitol is framed by the tower of the old Capitol on Wabasha and Exchange Streets and the spire of Central Presbyterian Church in this 1904 postcard view.

Photographs could be cheaply reproduced with new printing processes and sold as postcards for only one cent. St. Paulites could impress their friends and family back East, out West, or in the old country with colorized pictures showing their magnificent new Capitol overlooking downtown. Visitors purchased the postcards as keepsakes or mailed them back home to assure everyone that the train ride was fine or to show off their travels. "Wish you were here," they scribbled smugly.

In addition to postcards, objects decorated with likenesses of major attractions made good mementos of Minnesota. Commercial souvenirs froze memories in a tangible form. Since 1905 entrepreneurs have produced all kinds of State Capitol knickknacks; spoons, plates, cups, pillows, handkerchiefs, penholders, metal trays, and cigars are but a few early examples. Each was designed for reminiscing, but the souvenirs also spread the word about Minnesota's progress—a kind of boasting and boosting for the tourist and for the state.

Even fifty years after the Capitol was built, its image was as popular as ever. A model of the Capitol was wheeled down the streets of

The Capitol Room at Donaldson's department store was a popular 1950s lunch spot in St. Paul.

The Minnesota State Capitol was featured on such souvenirs as this 1915 ruffled cotton pillow cover.

Pulled up in front of the Capitol, this Minnesota centennial parade float in 1958 carried a miniature model of Cass Gilbert's elaborate statehouse.

St. Paul on a Minnesota-centennial parade float in 1958. Around the same time, the ladies who lunched at Donaldson's department store in downtown St. Paul sat in what was called the Capitol Room, beneath a giant photograph of the restaurant's namesake.

A SUITABLE INTERIOR

Progress on the Capitol between 1901 and 1905 had been a series of highs and lows. Recovery of the national economy from the depression of the 1890s had driven up the costs of materials and wages. Recognizing this problem, state legislators approved a $1 million increase in the funds in 1901. Then, building the dome proved more difficult than originally anticipated. It did not look like the original January 1903 completion deadline could be met.

If the project was going to be executed from start to finish in a manner befitting the great state of Minnesota, Gilbert and the board of commissioners had no choice but to ask for more time and more money. Channing Seabury reluctantly went back to the legislature in 1903 to request an additional $1.5 million. The money was eventually granted, but only after Gilbert and Seabury promised that the new Capitol would be ready for occupation absolutely no later than January 1, 1905.

The latest round of new funds went toward creating a first-class interior. Gilbert wanted the inside of the Capitol to mirror the splendor of its exterior. And it did. After the Georgia marble dispute, it was pretty much set in stone that local materials would be used for the interior. Gilbert had good luck with the stone he found in Minnesota. Its color was well suited to the overall interior design. An elegant pinkish Kasota limestone from Le Sueur County was chosen to line the walls of the rotunda and the stairwells. Eight columns of granite from Rockville and Ortonville surround the rotunda on the second level. Bands of red pipestone from Minnesota's southern prairies highlight the murals and the dome.

Only where Minnesota stone was not suitable was imported stone used. The two grand staircases leading from the rotunda to the second floor are made of marble from France. Marbles from Greece and Italy can be seen in the stairwells. And the thirty-six columns surrounding the stairwells on the second level are richly veined marble from Italy. The various stones give the interior a bejeweled appearance.

When it came to designing the interior, Cass Gilbert was commander in chief. He took a personal interest in all aspects of the building's design, including choosing the artists who would decorate the interior. With Gilbert in charge, Minnesota's showcase for the state would also become a showplace for America's leading muralists.

At the end of the nineteenth century, murals were important to, and reinforced the goals of, civic architecture. The leading muralists of the time developed lofty theories about how art could improve society: art would beautify public spaces, and, in turn, they thought, educate and uplift people through its beauty. Moreover, murals were a democratic form of art. Unlike framed paintings, they were accessible to everyone because they were part of the actual structure of public buildings.

Gilbert's roster of artists included some of the biggest names in American art of that era: Edward Simmons, Henry Walker, Edwin Blashfield, John LaFarge, and Kenyon Cox. They all hailed from the East, and some had

wanted artists who would attract attention. These were men whose murals adorned major buildings all over the United States. Hiring such figures would attest to the sophisticated tastes of Minnesotans.

GOPHERS AND MAIDENS

Celebrity artists were not the only painters Gilbert hired. Others were commercial decorators led by Elmer E. Garnsey from New York,

Thirty-six columns of motley Italian marble surround the walls of the grand stairways.

made their reputations as mural painters for the 1893 World's Columbian Exposition. Gilbert was criticized in some circles for not hiring local artists, but he wanted the big names with the most experience. He also

chief decorator of the mural painting at the Library of Congress. That Garnsey hired a local firm to do much of the actual work on the Capitol decorations quieted some of the criticism about using non-Minnesota artists.

A first-floor ceiling decoration, one in a series by Elmer Garnsey, features a five-pointed *L'Etoile du Nord*.

Garnsey was in charge of creating the Capitol's secondary decorations and working with Gilbert to determine color schemes for the walls and ceilings. In St. Paul, his designs adorn many surfaces of the Capitol's upper and lower levels. They represent Minnesota through familiar images: oak leaves, acorns, corn, wheat, and produce. Patterns of flowers and fruit cover the ceilings of the first floor. Garnsey's designs pay homage to the little everyday things that Minnesotans hold dear.

Gilbert also showed his appreciation for Minnesota's beloved symbols. He designed the life-size gophers in the iron grillwork of the first floor stairwell. The showy lady's slippers (the state flower) on the top section (capitals) of the interior columns were also his doing.

Centered on the floor of the rotunda is Gilbert's *Star of the North*, an inlaid design of brass and thick frosted glass. The eight points of the star form the letter M when seen from any angle. Other decorations in the Capitol were much harder to figure out.

Visitors to the Capitol on January 2, 1905, were enthusiastic about the murals that were already in place in the rotunda, the hallways, and the legislative chambers. The effect of the huge, prismatic globe illuminating the jewel-toned murals in the rotunda was especially spectacular. "Minnesota can well be proud of its new Capitol," announced a reporter for the *Minneapolis Tribune* shortly after the building was revealed. Then, as if to refocus Minnesotans enamored solely with the glitz and glamour of the new building, the same reporter reminded them that the Capitol was "not an art gallery." Nor, he said, was it "constructed for show or to satisfy the artistic sense of the designers or builders." His intention was to assure the public that the painted nymphs and exotic stones would not detract from the function of the Capitol as a house of government and a serious monument to the sovereignty of the state. The *Tribune* article read much like a guide to an art exhibition. It educated readers in the history and meaning of classical architecture. It told them to be impressed that America's foremost muralists were responsible for the "magnificent" decorations. And it tried to convince skeptics that the Capitol was indeed beautiful and appropriate to its purpose. In effect, the Minneapolis commentator gave the new Capitol a glowing review on opening night.

The gushing reporter was also the first public guide to the building. His words took the reader on a tour. Just as visitors to the Capitol today walk though the building with a guide who narrates its history, the meanings of the paintings, and details about the different types of stone, visitors in 1905 needed some assistance too. The first official guide to the Capitol was not published until 1907. Before that, the people of Minnesota relied on the newspapers to explain what they were seeing. This was especially necessary for Minnesotans unfamiliar with what is known as allegorical art.

American muralists during the nineteenth and early-twentieth centuries often painted stories

or characters from the classical past to represent ideas rather than specific places, events, or things. Instead of painting familiar scenes that might be easily recognizable, such as famous battles or well-known people, they painted ancient-looking figures to symbolize something else. For example, an image of a woman in flowing robes and a cap could stand for an idea such as liberty. These figures were not supposed to look like a particular person. They were idealized, which means they were the

Friendly gophers in the second-floor ironwork remind visitors why Minnesota is called the Gopher State. Prompted by a popular newspaper cartoon, Minnesotans in the middle of the 1800s chose prairie gophers—which are actually thirteen-striped ground squirrels—to represent their new state.

Winnowing, **a lunette by Elmer Garnsey, pays tribute to Minnesota's farmworkers.**

artist's idea of perfection. Allegorical painting, like beaux arts architecture, came from Europe, where American artists often went to study. Muralists of this era admired the great painters and masterpieces of the Renaissance, such as Michelangelo's ceiling in the Sistine Chapel.

As on the ceiling of the Sistine Chapel, it was not uncommon to see undressed or nude figures in American murals, especially female figures. The idealized human body was believed to be beautiful, and beauty, the artists said, was uplifting for the spirit. Paintings of nude women were not intended to be sexual or unseemly. They were meant to be inspiring and spiritual.

Many ordinary Americans thought this was ridiculous. Perhaps artists could get away with painting pictures of nudes in Europe, the common cry went, but not in America among

proper, God-fearing people! When challenged, however, supporters of allegory often fired off snobbish retorts about how uncultured and unsophisticated boors were unable to understand fine art. When Cass Gilbert was planning the interior of Minnesota's Capitol building, he did consider how the state's residents might react to nude or seminude figures painted on the ceiling and walls of their building. He decided, however, that Minnesotans were open-minded. The new Capitol, after all, was supposed to represent a Minnesota that was civilized and mature.

The State Capitol board was less certain. The commissioners asked Gilbert's artists not to "fill the building with Greek gods and goddesses." Likewise, one concerned citizen, the president of the Minnesota Historical Society and a veteran of the Civil War, publicly voiced his opposition to allegory. "We want no Greek or

Roman antiques, however classic, no dancing nymphs or goddesses on the walls of the Capitol," he said in 1903. "The desire is to have our own local history illustrated, our own battles, our own heroes, our own barbarians, our own lakes and rivers." In the face of this protest, however, the gods and goddesses of the ancient world still managed to find a home in Minnesota's Capitol.

Besides collaborating with Gilbert on the decorative floral designs for the walls and ceilings, Elmer Garnsey created allegorical figures for the Capitol. For the space below the skylight at the top of each grand staircase, he designed twelve paintings shaped like half-moons (called lunettes) to symbolize the state's industries and activities. Each painting shows one figure surrounded by clues about what the figure represents. For example, a woman who catches a stream of grain with a sack is *Milling*. Some of Garnsey's figures wear classical togas, but most are dressed in modern clothing typical of their activity. A few of them, such as *Winnowing*, look more like burly-armed Minnesota farm girls than Greek goddesses. They look to be local images that have been classed up a bit. Not all of the paintings are this viewer-friendly, however.

At the end of the skylight over the Supreme Court is a lunette painted by Kenyon Cox titled *The Contemplative Spirit of the East*. Cox was a prominent painter from New York who had studied art there and in Paris. His mural for Minnesota's Capitol shows three female figures. The figure in the center wears a large pair of purple wings. She rests her head on her hand in a pose of contemplation. She is "Thought." The figure on the left, "Letters," holds a book. The third figure, "Law," holds a bridle and a staff. All are dressed in ancient garb; one wears a laurel wreath on her head. Today, as in 1905, the meaning of the figures is hard to figure out without a guidebook. The mural is a nice decoration, but less satisfactory as a story pertinent to the lives of Minnesotans.

Cass Gilbert added lady's slippers to the capitals of marble columns on the second floor. The rare wildflower had recently been named the state flower in 1902. They grow in Minnesota's swamps, bogs, and damp wooded areas, but state law has made picking them illegal since 1925.

The Contemplative Spirit of the East by Kenyon Cox can be seen at the top of the staircase leading to the Supreme Court Chamber. The three women represent "Letters," "Thought," and "Law."

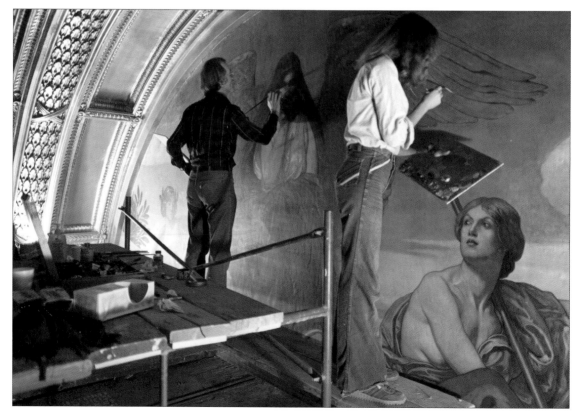

Professional art conservators clean and restore *The Contemplative Spirit of the East* in 1979.

THE ROTUNDA MURALS

Pride of place in Minnesota's Capitol was given to Edward H. Simmons. His four murals decorate the upper part of the rotunda. They are collectively titled *The Civilization of the Northwest* and represent the ideas of westward migration and the march of civilization. Rather than use classical figures to represent abstract ideas as Cox and Walker did, Simmons adapted classical imagery to a historical theme that Minnesotans could understand and learn from. Civilization on the march was a popular subject; westward movement was the theme chosen to decorate the House of Representatives of the U.S. Capitol in Washington, D.C. Another of the Minnesota Capitol's muralists, Edwin Blashfield, had painted a mural for the Library of Congress titled *The Evolution of Civilization.* He would finish another mural, *Westward,* for the Iowa State Capitol in 1904.

Each of Simmons's panels in the rotunda is twenty-nine feet long and thirteen feet wide. According to an early guidebook, the first depicts a young man, the "American Spirit," leaving his home in the East. Two figures, "Timidity" and "Convention," attempt to hold him back, but he is guided by "Hope" (in green) and "Wisdom" (with the helmet), who will accompany him throughout his journey. In the second panel, the young man rids the land of cowardice, savagery, sin, and stupidity, each represented by an animal or semi-human beast. The third panel shows the same young man breaking ground on the frontier by lifting a large rock. The last in the sequence represents the final phase of the young man's journey. He sits on a throne like a Roman god, commanding the winds to disperse the products of his state. A loaf of bread is carried off by the gusting winds. One female figure holds a small model of Gilbert's Capitol that will spread the art and culture of Minnesota throughout the world. The picture represents Minnesota's rise to civilization.

Simmons's panels have all the drama of a full-blown Hollywood epic. Without some sort of explanation or guidebook, viewers will not know the names of the main characters or exactly what they are doing in each panel, but it is not too hard to grasp the general idea. Solving the puzzle is part of the fun of looking at this type of classical art.

The Civilization of the Northwest was actually painted in Simmons's studio in Paris. When each section was complete, the artist removed the painted canvas from its wooden support, rolled it up, and sent it on a boat across the Atlantic Ocean. After a lengthy train ride from the East Coast, the murals arrived in St. Paul, where they were unrolled and pasted onto the curved spaces of the upper rotunda.

One of Simmons's paintings nearly met an undignified end on an unusually hot day in September 1912. The glue melted and the mural fell two stories onto the rotunda floor—as if St. Paul's Vulcans were demonstrating their opinion of allegorical art. The next month another panel dropped. Neither painting was damaged, and both were pasted back on the ceiling, where they have remained ever since.

The Civilization of the Northwest, four murals by Edward H. Simmons, adorn the dome of the rotunda.

Portions of these murals can be seen in upper corners of the photograph of the rotunda on page 44.

THE SENATE MURALS

The Senate Chamber is home to Edwin Blashfield's lunette murals, *The Discoverers and Civilizers Led to the Source of the Mississippi* and *Minnesota—Granary of the World*. When Cass Gilbert first met with his chosen artists he suggested some appropriate subjects for their paintings. None of the artists were from Minnesota, and all of them would paint the murals in faraway studios and then ship the finished paintings to St. Paul. Like Simmons, Blashfield approached his subject with a mix of local history and classical idealism. Both murals contain figures in the drapery of the ancient world mixed with others in costumes appropriate to the characters they depict.

The seated central figure in *The Discoverers and Civilizers Led to the Source of the Mississippi* is a Native American, "the Great Spirit of Manitou, Father of the Waters." He pours the Mississippi River from a large jar. At the right, "the Spirit of Discovery," a winged woman, guides seventeenth-century French explorers and traders. The group on the right shows a priest and the early settlers watched over by "the Spirit of Civilization." A Native American wearing a warrior's headdress challenges the explorers to his right. The priest on the left offers salvation to the young Indian girl at the feet of Manitou.

Across the room, Blashfield's other mural, *Minnesota—Granary of the World*, represents the progress of Minnesota since the days of the Civil War. The central figure, on a harvest cart full of wheat pulled by two white oxen, represents Minnesota. Two winged females place a crown of victory upon her head. The spirit of patriotism hovers over the group representing 1861 at the right—soldiers, a drummer boy, and a nurse. On the left, men and women in contemporary dress surrounded by symbols of industry and agriculture represent a peaceful and prosperous Minnesota in the new century. The artist honored his patrons, Cass Gilbert and Channing Seabury, by including their faces in the picture. Theirs are the two closest to the left edge of the canvas.

Together, Blashfield's murals represent the progress of Minnesota from the primitive days of exploration to its turn-of-the-century greatness. These themes echo throughout the State Capitol. Daniel Chester French and Edward C. Potter's quadriga also represents the idea of progress. So do Simmons's panels in the rotunda. Images of this type present a version of history that is meant to inspire Minnesotans to take pride in their accomplishments and to continue their energetic push into the future.

The Capitol's artistic program triggered both shock and awe. Some Minnesotans continued to insist that the story of the state was better told through exact events, dates, and heroes rather than symbolic figures that people often couldn't recognize. In 1910, one ornery critic took offense with the golden quadriga and urged Minnesotans to "take a sledge hammer and smash 'them' Roman bronchos and that chariot! Clean 'em out and put a grand heroic statue of Alexander Ramsey in their stead!" No one did, of course.

Edwin Blashfield's *Minnesota—Granary of the World* decorates the Senate Chamber.

Over the past century, the style and decoration of Gilbert's building has fallen in and out of favor. Some people have a taste for it, and some find the "beauty pile" overly pretentious for Minnesota. But today, as in 1905, visitors walk up and down the marble stairways "drinking in the beauties of the decorations." And it is still possible to buy souvenir plates, spoons, cups, and postcards depicting the Capitol that stands proudly for Minnesota.

The Discoverers and Civilizers Led to the Source of the Mississippi, also by Edwin Blashfield.

What's a Quadriga?

A quadriga is a four-horse chariot from the ancient world. The Greeks often portrayed their gods and goddesses riding in them. In later Roman times, quadrigas carrying victorious emperors or generals were depicted on coins, buildings, and public monuments to commemorate military triumphs and the peace that followed.

The quadriga at the base of the dome of Minnesota's State Capitol is one of the most recognizable features of the building. Officially titled *The Progress of the State*, it includes an athletic-looking man standing triumphantly in a chariot. The chariot is guided by two women who hold the reins of four spirited steeds. The man represents "Minnesota," the word written on the banner he holds aloft. In his right arm he carries a horn of plenty that overflows with the bounties of a good harvest. The horses signify the powers of nature: Air, Fire, Water, and Earth. The women are allegories of "Industry" and "Agriculture." The group represents a successful Minnesota, its prosperity, and its good government.

Daniel Chester French of Massachusetts and his student, Edward C. Potter of Connecticut, designed this group of statuary. It is made of ten thousand pounds of copper and steel, covered in thin sheets of real gold, and cost $35,000, an enormous sum for the times.

French was one of the preeminent sculptors in America. His best-known work is the heroic statue of Abraham Lincoln in the Lincoln Memorial in Washington, D.C. Potter had made a name for himself as a sculptor of animals, and went on to sculpt the famous marble lions outside the New York Public Library. Dividing the work on Minnesota's quadriga, French designed the figures and Potter was responsible for the horses. French also created the figures that stand on the ledge below the quadriga: *Wisdom, Prudence, Courage,*

Daniel Chester French's *Prudence*.

60

Minnesota's quadriga, *The Progress of the State*, by Daniel Chester French and Edward C. Potter, is the crowning glory of the State Capitol.

Daniel Chester French and Edward C. Potter designed a Columbus quadriga for the 1893 World's Columbian Exposition in Chicago.

Bounty, Truth, and *Integrity.* These statues represent the six virtues that support the progress of Minnesota. The artists sculpted smaller clay models of the statues in their studios. These models were shipped to St. Paul, where skilled craftsmen reproduced the full-sized versions from permanent materials.

French and Potter had collaborated on their first quadriga for the 1893 World's Columbian Exposition in Chicago. It crowned a monumental arch of triumph within the "White City." This statuary group featured a fourteen-

Sculptor Daniel Chester French works on a bust in his Massachusetts studio. Behind French is his model of Abraham Lincoln for the Lincoln Memorial in Washington, D.C.

foot-high Christopher Columbus standing in a four-horse chariot guided by two maidens. On either side of the chariot, two mounted attendants carried staffs of victory. The group was called *The Triumph of Columbus*.

French and Potter began work on Minnesota's quadriga group in 1903. When the Capitol was dedicated in 1905, it was not yet in place. It was hoisted up the very next year with much fanfare and its own dedication ceremony. The

This label for Minneapolis-made Le Nord cigars features Minnesota's golden quadriga, ca. 1906.

Cass Gilbert saw this quadriga group in Chicago, and by 1897 he was making plans to have French and Potter adapt it for Minnesota. The fact that the quadriga was associated with the Chicago Fair helped to underscore the sophistication of the new building in St. Paul.

quadriga was gilded on site until it gleamed bright in the sun. Vulnerable to the elements, it received needed repair and regilding in 1949 and 1979. During 1994–1995, the statuary was removed from the Capitol for complete restoration and regilding.

Solemn St. Paul schoolgirls form a "living flag" for the Flag Day parade of 1905.

chapter four

Celebrating & Commemorating

THE SCHOOLGIRLS *who dressed up in red, white, and blue capes and hats on June 14, 1905, were well coached in the patriotic pageantry of St. Paul. "Living flags" had been regular features of parades in their city and throughout the United States since the 1890s.*

The girls quickly fell into formation on the Exchange Street steps of the old Capitol. Forty-eight students wore blue capes and white star hats for the forty-eight states. The rest, in red and white capes, formed straight lines for the thirteen stripes of Old Glory. After posing for a photo, the living-flag girls led the veteran color guard that carried the battle flags of the Civil War and the Spanish-American War from the old Capitol to the rotunda of the new Capitol building.

For Minnesota's Civil War veterans this was a day of reunion. They had met at the old Capitol and taken roll, remembering those who had died since last they met. "Never, perhaps, since, as dashing young fellows they were first mustered in and sent to join Lincoln's armies, have there been so many regiments of the Civil War assembled in one place," one newspaper reported.

Special railroad rates had been arranged to help bring home the "old boys" who had dispersed throughout the West. One traveled "all the way from Idaho to meet with his comrades again," a reporter noted. The same journalist opined that the "grizzled veterans" were "flirting with death" by marching in the parade. But it was an important occasion, and the chance to honor their role in Minnesota history outweighed the risks.

At exactly one-thirty in the afternoon, with military precision, the gray-haired regiments of the Civil War and the recently battle-tested units of the Spanish-American and Philippine Wars filed out of the old Capitol and onto the lawn. The flag bearers entered the old rotunda, where Colonel C. T. Trowbridge threw open the glass display cases and presented each color guard with one treasured battle flag. Many flags were torn and tattered, not much more than strips of colored silk attached to their staffs. But the guards handled them with loving care and answered their calls by snapping salutes to the former Civil War officer. The flags of the First through Tenth Regiments of Minnesota, the Second Cavalry, and the First Artillery were delivered to the bearers.

The march from the old Capitol to the new began promptly at two o'clock. The living flag led the Minnesota regiments to Rice Park, where they were joined by more schoolchildren, marching bands, and floats. A group of Navy men rode on a float decorated to look like the *U.S.S. Minnesota*—not a copy of the wooden steam frigate from the Civil War, but the new sixteen-thousand-ton battleship *Minnesota* that had been launched just two months earlier off the coast of Virginia. The newspapers reported that ten thousand people marched up Cedar Street through downtown St. Paul to the "magnificent marble pile on the hill."

The procession stopped at the steps of the new Capitol. The living flag girls stepped aside and saluted as the old veterans delivered their flags to a stand set up for the speeches. The state band played the "Star-Spangled Banner," and Archbishop John Ireland of St. Paul, once the chaplain of the Fifth Minnesota, committed the flags to the care of the state on behalf of the veterans. Accepting the flags, Governor John A. Johnson summed up the weighty meaning of the threadbare banners, lest it be lost amid the festivities: "Monuments might tell the story of your [the veterans'] patriotism, but no marble shaft could so well tell the story of

Civil War and Spanish-American War veterans proudly transfer their battle flags from the old Capitol to the new statehouse on Flag Day, June 14, 1905.

The battleship *U.S.S. Minnesota* sails as a float in the Flag Day parade of 1905.

your valor and chivalry as those drooping standards under whose folds you marched into the very jaws of death that this land might be 'the land of the free and the home of the brave.'" At the conclusion of Johnson's speech, the battle flags of two wars were carried up the steps and deposited into the four bronze and glass cases in the rotunda of the new State Capitol, where they remain today.

The ideal mingles with the actual in the rotunda's battle flags. They are tangible reminders of episodes in Minnesota's history too near in the minds of its living veterans in 1905 to be recounted through the highbrow classical figures that hovered above them in Edward Simmons's westward-migration murals.

As Cass Gilbert was making plans in 1903 for a decorative program for the Capitol, a few Minnesota interest groups weighed in on the subject. Given their druthers, Minnesota's veterans would have done away with the Greek gods and goddesses. What they wanted for the Capitol were real-to-life pictures commemorating their own heroism in battle. The Governor's Reception Room became the place for this, and in the years that followed, patriotic citizens' groups planned more conventional honors for the rotunda.

WOMEN'S CONTRIBUTIONS

Despite its increases, the budget for the Capitol did not allow for embellishment of every sculptural niche or wall. Many were empty when the building was occupied. The State Capitol board of commissioners was content to leave the vacant spaces for later generations of Minnesotans to fill. During the first few decades of the twentieth century, civic-minded citizens groups filled some of those spaces with commemorative statues and plaques. In recent years, the desire to retain the historic integrity of the building has dampened zeal for additions to the interior of the building. Nonetheless, a few important memorials to modern-

day heroes have been commissioned for the first floor, such as a sculptural portrait in bronze of Martin Luther King Jr.

Cass Gilbert hoped to remain an artistic consultant at the Capitol, but once the project was completed and the board disbanded, he no longer had control over what went into the building. The architect was awakened to this reality in 1909. Gilbert wanted to fill the empty niches on the second level of the rotunda with sculptures by big-name artists, men of international repute like those he had hired to design the murals. But the citizens group in charge of assigning the commission for a sculpture of Colonel William Colvill instead chose Catherine F. Backus of Minneapolis.

Colonel Colvill had led the charge of the First Minnesota at Gettysburg. He died on the eve of the Flag Day celebration in June 1905 and was the first person to lie in state in the rotunda of the new Capitol. He was a Minnesota hero. Gilbert did not hold his tongue on the matter of the commission.

"You now have before you models for this important work by persons who are naturally ambitious but who, so far as I can ascertain, utterly lack the training and experience to execute the work," he warned the citizens group. They ignored his advice. The larger-than-life likeness of Colvill was cast in bronze and placed in a rotunda niche. Gilbert continued to withhold his blessing for that "damned bad statue," as he called it. Others liked it. In 1928 President Calvin Coolidge dedicated a replica

Battle flags from several wars are preserved in the rotunda of the Capitol.

of the statue in Colvill's hometown of Cannon Falls, Minnesota.

Gilbert had a reputation for being pompous at times. He did not see the potential of Minnesota's art community when he chose the muralists for the most visible spaces of the Capitol, nor did he see it in 1909. That a local sculptor (a woman!) was chosen for the project ruffled the architect's feathers. It was unusual for a woman to make a career as a professional artist in 1909. But Catherine Backus was not the only woman in Minneapolis and St. Paul who worked in the arts. Enrollment at the Minneapolis School of Art was predominantly female, and a number of art and craft groups were founded by women for the purpose of exhibiting and selling their work. Backus took her work very seriously, even if Gilbert did not. The rest of the bronze war heroes in the other rotunda niches were not to his taste either.

Backus also designed a bronze memorial plaque to the First Minnesota Volunteer Infantry, which is mounted on a wall between the battle flag cases on the Capitol's first floor. Executed in bas relief—a sculptural style by which the figures are partially raised from a flat tablet—Backus's plaque is educational and affecting. The five colonels of the First Minnesota, all in uniform, are represented on the left side of the plaque. On the right in flowing drapery is a tall woman (probably representing "Victory") and a young boy in breeches holding a flag. The figures flank a written history of the regiment and an account of their battles. The other memorial of this type in the rotunda is a busy bas-relief

Catherine Backus's statue of Minnesota Civil War hero Colonel William Colvill raised the ire of Cass Gilbert.

69

tablet recounting the battles of the Spanish-American War and the Philippine Insurrection. The sculpture was created by Brioschi Studios of St. Paul.

Women are often said to be the keepers of culture. During the first half of the twentieth century, the public aspirations of many women were played out through social groups and

Governor Theodore Christianson and Alexander Ramsey's daughter Marion Ramsey Furness (with her daughters, Anita, left, and Laura) dedicate a plaque in the late Governor Ramsey's honor in 1929.

civic activities. Women's groups were often responsible for organizing and raising funds for public memorials. In 1929 the National Society of the Colonial Dames of America and Minnesota governor Theodore Christianson dedicated a large bronze plaque to Alexander Ramsey (now outside the governor's office), the first territorial governor of Minnesota and the second governor of the state. Minnesota's founding father was the *real* father and grandfather of these Colonial Dames, who, of course, determined which person they would commemorate in the Capitol.

There are also two bronze tablets in the rotunda honoring the accomplishments of Minnesota women. Louise Cross sculpted a plaque dedicated to Clara H. Ueland, a leader of the women's suffrage movement in Minnesota. Ueland was also a member of the State Art Society and Handicrafts Guild. Dr. Martha G. Ripley was another Minnesotan instrumental in persuading legislators and other elected officials to support suffrage for women. A bronze plaque by the Minnesota artist Charles S. Wells commemorates Ripley's work as a "pioneering woman physician" and founder of a maternity hospital in Minneapolis. As the building was nearing completion in 1903, one more space in the Capitol was set aside for remembering Minnesotans.

THE CIVIL WAR SCENES

When Cass Gilbert submitted his plans for Capitol decorations to the State Capitol board of commissioners in 1903, he intended to keep the Governor's Reception Room relatively plain. That is not how it turned out. Local groups quickly made known their wishes to have Minnesota history clearly illustrated somewhere in the Capitol—without Greek gods or goddesses. Representing the Minnesota Historical Society, James H. Baker suggested the theme of the treaty of the Traverse des Sioux. Archbishop John Ireland recommended Father Hennepin discovering the Falls of St. Anthony. The Civil War veterans wanted specific battles memorialized as well. Gilbert warned Channing Seabury that if the board of commissioners did not make plans for the blank spaces in the Governor's Reception Room, then "somebody will get in their deadly political work later on and make that room a chamber of horrors in the name of patriotism." Gilbert immediately went to work planning more pictures.

The Governor's Reception Room, located in the west end of the building, serves as a place for conferences and for the governor to meet with the public. The look of the room is supposedly Venetian, but most see it as just fancy. With its wainscoted walls, gilded carvings, ironwork M's, velvet curtains, and stuffed leather club chairs, the reception room is heavier and more ornate than the rest of the State Capitol. You can almost smell the cigars and brandy of the old days. And unlike the allegorical murals in the legislative chambers and the rotunda, the murals here illustrate specific people, places, and historical events. The descriptive paintings in the reception room were called murals, but they were really more akin to the large-scale easel paintings that would typically be hung on a wall rather than to the decorative murals elsewhere in the Capitol.

Accepting some suggestions put forth by the interest groups, Gilbert assigned the artists the themes to be depicted in the Governor's Reception Room. The architect met with several Minnesota veterans to determine appropriate subjects for a series of murals depicting the state's involvement in the Civil War.

Archbishop Ireland and James Baker from the Minnesota Historical Society also had their proposals approved. Four of the six paintings in the Governor's Reception Room are Civil War themes. Two others, by Edwin Blashfield (whose two lunettes decorate the Senate Chamber) and Stanley M. Arthurs, are situated in the entryway to the room.

The artists Gilbert commissioned to create canvases for the four spaces on the two long walls

Cass Gilbert commissioned Francis Davis Millet to paint *Father Hennepin Discovering the Falls of St. Anthony* for the Governor's Reception Room. The fancy decor of this room, which is unlike any other Capitol space, has been described as Venetian.

For *The Battle of Gettysburg,* Gilbert chose artist Rufus Zogbaum, who had made a specialty of painting military and naval subjects. His epic painting depicts a bloody moment of glory. Despite tremendous casualties, the heroic First Minnesota Regiment halted a Confederate advance at Gettysburg in 1863.

in the Governor's Reception Room were well respected and experienced. But each painter tackled his theme in his own style. Rufus H. Zogbaum, a military artist of some renown, was given the task of depicting the First Minnesota at the Battle of Gettysburg. The focus of his picture is a bright shell blast around which Colonel William Colvill's troops charge into the line of fire. There is a lot of space between the viewer and the action. The figures are arranged in a horizontal band that runs through the middle of the painting. Only a discarded knapsack and a dying soldier draw the eye into the distant, chaotic scene.

In Howard Pyle's *The Battle of Nashville,* the boys in blue of the Fifth, Seventh, Ninth, and Tenth Minnesota Regiments seem to charge over a hill and straight out of the picture. The hill slopes toward the viewer to allow an up-close look at the action and the fierce

Howard Pyle's *The Battle of Nashville,* another Civil War–themed painting in the Governor's Reception Room, also depicts Minnesota's involvement in the conflict. The Fifth, Seventh, Ninth, and Tenth Minnesota Regiments fought in the battle.

determination on the soldiers' faces. Rifles, bayonets, and ragged battle flags stick up at various dynamic angles.

Pyle was the leading illustrator of his day. He wrote and illustrated books and articles for popular magazines. He also mentored many young American illustrators, Stanley M. Arthurs among them, at his studio in Brandywine, Pennsylvania. Pyle was famous for making viewers eyewitnesses to the dramatic stories he told in his images—which is exactly what he did in *The Battle of Nashville*. The author of an early guidebook to the Capitol heaped praise upon the artist and his picture for Minnesota: "If Mr. Pyle never made another picture he would be considered a great artist."

Though Cass Gilbert may not have been interested in Minnesota's arts community, one of the artists he chose to paint two images for the Governor's Reception Room did have a local connection. In 1886, a group of art-minded Minneapolitans banded together to form the Minneapolis School of Art (now the Minneapolis College of Art and Design). Douglas Volk, an easterner who had studied in Paris, was the school's first director. Volk had been back in New York for more than a decade when Gilbert commissioned him for the Capitol paintings. The artist's earlier Minneapolis connection probably pleased the locals nonetheless.

MINNESOTA HISTORY
The first of two paintings Volk contributed to the Governor's Reception Room is an account of the battle at Mission Ridge, in which the Second Minnesota Regiment charged up a hill in the face of enemy fire. Volk was a stickler for accurate details. Part of his preparation was to visit the battlefield in Tennessee. Francis Davis Millet, the artist of the fourth Civil War panel, *The Fourth Minnesota Regiment Entering Vicksburg*, had firsthand knowledge of the war. He was a veteran of more than forty battles. Coincidentally, his was the only peaceful Civil War scene in the room.

Douglas Volk's second painting for the Capitol, *Father Hennepin at the Falls of St. Anthony*, occupies one end of the Governor's Reception Room. It was a popular scene in Minnesota lore; John K. Daniels, who carved the butter Capitol for the 1901 Pan-American Exposition, had later sculpted Father Louis Hennepin and his guides in butter for the 1904 Minnesota State Fair. Father Hennepin was a Belgian friar and an explorer in the service of France.

When Father Hennepin reached the Falls of St. Anthony in 1683, he named the site after St. Anthony of Padua. The Catholic friar was also an early enthusiast of the Upper Mississippi. Upon his return to France he wrote a best-selling book in which he described the Falls of St. Anthony as dropping more than fifty feet—about thirty-five feet more than they really did!

In Volk's painting, Father Hennepin holds a crucifix aloft to christen the falls. A group comprised of one other European explorer (Picard du Gay) and four Native Americans witnesses the blessing, some more attentively than others.

At the right, a half-dressed Native American woman carries a bundle of blankets into the scene on her back. The Native Americans are depicted as assistants to the explorers; one even looks up adoringly at Father Hennepin from his seat at the friar's feet. Two in the group, however, look somewhat suspicious of the two more reverent Native Americans.

As he did for his Vicksburg image, Volk researched the historical costumes of his sub-jects to give his picture authenticity. He is said to have also studied a portrait of Father Hennepin owned by railroad magnate James J. Hill of St. Paul. And there were plenty of doc-umentary images of Native Americans in books and journals. The photograph and postcard industry that produced so many images of the Minnesota State Capitol also turned out thou-sands of popular studio images of costumed Native Americans. Often, though, commercial photographers posed them in the dress of tribes

Father Hennepin at the Falls of St. Anthony **by Douglas Volk was Archbishop John Ireland's choice for the Governor's Reception Room. The artist faithfully replicated details of the characters' period clothing after careful historical research.**

other than their own. Such photographers sought to make exotic curiosities they could sell rather than historical records.

Artist Francis Davis Millet was assigned to fulfill the wishes of the Minnesota Historical Society with a painting depicting the signing of the Treaty of Traverse des Sioux, which occupies the other end of the Governor's Reception Room, opposite Volk's *Father Hennepin* (see page 16). The 1851 treaty between the U.S. government and the Sioux, which took place along the Minnesota River near present-day St. Peter, opened twenty-four million acres of Minnesota, Iowa, and North and South Dakota to white settlement. In return for their land, the Sioux were promised cash and annuities. They did not receive most of the payment, however. This sparked an uprising in 1862 that began three decades of intermittent warfare between the United States and the Plains Indians. Millet's painting does not tell this part of the story.

Earlier accounts and pictures place the signing of the Treaty of Traverse des Sioux under a canopied ceremonial platform built for the occasion. Millet is said to have built a similar leaf-covered canopy in his backyard to use as a visual reference as he painted. A crowd of Sioux, decked out in blankets and feather headdresses, commands the right side of the picture. A group of white settlers takes up the space on the left. Territorial governor Alexander Ramsey stands on the platform holding the medals to be given to each chief upon signing the treaty. The two sides are joined by the handshake between

a Sioux chief and U.S. Indian Commissioner Luke Lea.

Life on the frontier, however, was not always portrayed as so chivalrous. There were plenty of popular examples that presented a less peaceable image. The pulp magazine industry (named for the cheap paper used for printing) romanticized the exploits of the heroes and villains of the American West. Throughout the second half of the nineteenth century, popular magazines printed fictionalized accounts of the frontiersman (and later statesman) Davy Crockett, "the man in the coonskin cap" who went into battle with his fierce Indian foes. At the time when Volk and Millet were painting their historical scenes, dime novels and weekly magazines told gripping tales of western adventure, war parties, and brutal massacres at the hands of natives. The cover illustrations often showed violent struggles that alluded to the potboiler tales within.

This type of magazine made a media star out of William F. "Buffalo Bill" Cody, a plainsman and U.S. Army scout turned showman. "The public knows my brother as a boy Indian-slayer, a champion buffalo-hunter, a brave soldier, a daring scout, an intrepid frontiersman, and a famous exhibitor," wrote his sister, Helen Cody Wetmore, in 1899 from Codyview, her home in Duluth, Minnesota. A dime novelist of the 1880s serialized Buffalo Bill's exploits and encouraged him to take his stories to the stage, which he did in 1883. His immensely popular "Wild West Show" traveled throughout the United States and Europe. The show included reenactments of the Plains Indian Wars. Cody hired actual Native Americans to play the bad guys. It was this highly dramatized and one-sided version of history that most Americans knew best.

While paintings in the Governor's Reception Room do not depict the overdramatized, popular version of western history from pulp magazines and traveling shows, the scenes chosen for Minnesota's Capitol do tell only one side of the story. That side was the one taught to, or experienced by, the men who built the Capitol—the ones who got the land and those who fought the wars on the winning sides. It was not until much later in the twentieth century that it became common to question how history should be presented to the public. Since 1905, more people have begun to figure out how to tell a more balanced story.

Minnesota's Capitol is not just about commemorating the past, however. It is the seat of government for the state, the place where laws that determine Minnesota's future are made. And amid all the celebrating and commemorating that was going on in 1905, there was much business to attend to.

Minnesota legislators take a break from their daily bill-writing and lawmaking in the Senate Chamber, ca. 1905. Despite its artistically beautiful surroundings, the Capitol is first and foremost a place of state business.

The Flag of the Twenty-Eighth Virginia

Minnesota soldiers gave their lives in the Civil War and the Spanish-American War to protect the battle flags now enshrined in the rotunda of the Minnesota State Capitol. Some of the flags now carefully preserved in bronze and glass cases were no more than tattered silk remnants when carried from the battlefields. Even so, what was left symbolized the valor and sacrifice of Minnesota's soldiers. For the veterans who carried the flags up the hill from the old Capitol to the new Capitol in June 1905, it was a point of pride to preserve their history.

Battle flags are the pride of any military unit; it is an honor to bear the colors in battle. It is also an honor to capture an enemy flag. For a Union soldier in the Civil War, capturing the flag of a Confederate regiment earned him a Congressional Medal of Honor. In 1905 one Civil War battle flag, a captured Rebel flag, was not

War flags on display in the rotunda.

transferred to the new Capitol from its place in the old Capitol. Some veterans felt that it would be unseemly to prominently display a Confederate flag in the rotunda of the new Capitol. In fact, the rightful home of this flag has been in dispute for more than 140 years.

The story told in Minnesota starts with a soldier of the First Minnesota Volunteer Infantry, Private Marshall Sherman. On July 3, 1863, he was one of the soldiers in the Union Army of the Potomac at Gettysburg who surged over a ridge to drive back the Rebel army on the march toward Philadelphia. Out of the horror and chaos of battle, Sherman emerged carrying the flag of the Twenty-Eighth Virginia Infantry. Legend has him holding a bayonet to the chest of a Confederate flag bearer and ordering him to "throw down that flag or I'll run you through!"

St. Paul artist John A. Weide recorded for posterity the deteriorating battle flags on display in the second Minnesota State Capitol in 1895. His series of twenty-six paintings includes this image of the flag of the Twenty-Eighth Virginia.

The flag of the Twenty-Eighth Virginia was put into storage with other captured banners in the War Department in Washington. Talk of returning the flags began in 1887, but President Grover Cleveland rebuffed the suggestion. Congress, however, requested an inventory of the captured flags. The flag of the Twenty-Eighth Virginia was recorded as being on loan. It is likely that it had been taken to Minnesota as a war trophy in 1864 to help drum up patriotic sentiment and new Union Army recruits. While in St. Paul, however, the flag fell into the hands of Marshall Sherman, the man who had captured it at Gettysburg. It was never returned to Washington.

Congress passed an act in 1905 stating that all captured Civil War flags in the War Department were to be returned to their respective states. The flag of the Twenty-Eighth Virginia was not in the War Department, however. It was in the possession of a veterans organization housed in the old Capitol building in St. Paul—and they were determined to keep it. In 1901 veterans of the Confederate Army from Mississippi requested the return of two Rebel flags captured in 1864 by the

Marshall Sherman poses with his prize.

Fourth Minnesota. The legal opinion of Minnesota's attorney general was that the flags belonged to the veterans and did not have to be returned. The Fourth Minnesota entrusted its trophies to the Minnesota Historical Society in 1905. But the veterans of the First Minnesota kept their treasured flag of the Twenty-Eighth Virginia in their offices in the old Capitol. It remained there until it was given to the Minnesota Historical Society in 1923.

That, however, is not the end of the story. In 1998 a group of Civil War reenactors from Roanoke, Virginia, asked that the Minnesota Historical Society return the Confederate flag. Theirs was the first of many requests to be refused. "Absolutely not! I mean, why? We won," Governor Jesse Ventura responded in 2000. In July 2004 Governor Mark Warner of Virginia talked about taking up the matter with Governor Tim Pawlenty. But 142 years after the Civil War battle in which Marshall Sherman deflagged the Twenty-Eighth Virginia, Minnesota has no plans to undo his deed. And Virginia, for its part, has no plans to stop asking.

Governor John A. Johnson with his wife, Elinore, and their much beloved dog
Ray, ca. 1905. St. Paul named a high school for Governor Johnson, where Wendell
Anderson, governor of Minnesota from 1971 to 1976, attended classes. Recently
renovated and repurposed, John A. Johnson High School is now John A. Johnson
Achievement Plus Elementary School.

chapter five

Business on the Hill

JOHN ALBERT JOHNSON *was the first native Minnesotan to become governor of the state. This born-in-a-log-cabin Democrat was also the first Minnesota governor to serve in the new Capitol.*

On the morning of January 4, 1905, Johnson's inauguration packed the House Chamber. The room brimmed with state legislators, distinguished visitors, and a public audience that took up every available seat in the viewing galleries. After being sworn in by the chief justice, the new governor took to the podium to speak; his oratory talents would make him one of Minnesota's most popular figures. Johnson outlined his progressive platform on many things of concern to Minnesotans in 1905, from busting big business to improving dairy farming.

Then outgoing Governor Samuel Van Sant stepped up to the speaker's stand to bid his farewell to the rewards and trials of office. That evening, one newspaper reported, the members of his "executive family" gave Van Sant a "very fine" davenport to thank him for his loyal service to the state.

Although Minnesota's Capitol is indeed an impressive showplace, perfect for pomp and ceremony, most of what goes on inside is not glamorous. The building is a place of governmental business. If there was one fault to Cass Gilbert's Capitol design, it was that there was not enough space for business. Up until 1932, when the State Office Building was constructed, numerous civic functions were housed inside the Capitol. Minnesotans even went there to get their drivers' licenses. Many have said that Gilbert was more concerned with the grandiose look of Minnesota's Capitol than with its function. But the building was (and is) magnificent, and its appearance spoke plenty about what it was all about and what went on there.

Most state governments have three branches: the executive, the legislative, and the judicial. The governor of a state is the head of the executive branch. Minnesota's governor has his office in the Capitol. The three chambers that radiate from the central rotunda—the House of Representatives, the Senate, and the Supreme Court—are where the lawmakers (legislators) and those who enforce the laws (judges) preside. The layout of the building is a

Sixty-seven adults and forty-six children representing twenty-six countries become U.S. citizens in the House Chamber of the Capitol on Citizenship Day, 1976.

visual expression of the separate powers of democratic government. But the tall dome of Minnesota's Capitol, like all domes in American civic architecture, is a unifying symbol.

The dramatic dome of the U.S. Capitol in Washington, D.C., the prototype for so many state capitol domes at the end of the nineteenth century, is the consummate symbol for American democracy. It is a visualization of the nation's motto, *E Pluribus Unum* ("Out of Many, One"). Under the dome of the federal Capitol, the fifty states and all American citizens are symbolically united. President Abraham Lincoln recognized the power of such a symbol during the Civil War.

The U.S. Capitol has had an eventful history, beginning from the moment George Washington laid the cornerstone in 1793. It has been built, torched, rebuilt, extended, and restored. When the building was first nearing completion, redcoats of the British Army set fire to it during the War of 1812. By 1829, it had been rebuilt with a disappointingly low dome. In 1855 President Millard Fillmore commissioned Thomas Ustick Walter of Philadelphia to design a bigger, better dome. It was not yet finished when war broke out between the states. During the depths of the Civil War, President Lincoln had the builders press on to finish the dome. "If people see the Capitol going on," he reasoned, "it is a sign we intend the Union shall go on." The U.S. Capitol's soaring white dome (which is not marble but painted iron) was finished in December 1863. It immediately became a

sorely needed patriotic symbol for the Union. Even those Americans who never visited Washington, D.C., came to know and love the Capitol dome and its meaning through popular photographs and prints.

MINNESOTA UNITED AND DIVIDED

The postcards and photographs of Minnesota's Capitol that went into production around 1904 had a result similar to that of the U.S. Capitol pictures that circulated after the Civil War. For Americans who had grown up with the symbolism of democracy, Minnesota's Capitol looked familiar. For immigrants, it was a tangible reminder of why they had come to America. In far-flung towns like Roseau or Montevideo, Minnesotans who may never have been to St. Paul knew that they were represented by the shining new Capitol in the picture postcards. And some even made the trip to the "big city" just to see the famous building. From the citizens who gathered on Wabasha Hill to witness the groundbreaking nearly a decade earlier to those who meandered up and down the marble stairways, admiring the decorations as soon as the building opened, Minnesotans felt a connection to *their* Capitol.

The Capitol is a place where Minnesotans come together. It can be an attractive backdrop, as it was for many years when the St. Paul Winter Carnival held its festivities in the park area right in front of the building. The ice palace of 1937 looked nearly as big as the Capitol.

In 1917, during World War I, wooden bleachers were built over the Capitol steps for a patriotic

St. Paulites frolic on the Capitol grounds during Winter Carnival festivities in 1917.

meeting. Speeches were given and songs sung by women's groups in a show of support for the soldiers "over there." Then as now, the Capitol was a place to rally in a show of solidarity and to find comfort in numbers. On September 16, 2001, five days after the September 11 tragedy, thirty-five thousand people gathered under gray skies on the Capitol grounds in St. Paul for "Minnesota Remembers: A Memorial from the Heartland." It was the largest assembly at the Capitol in recent memory, and one of many memorials like it at state capitols all over America. People of varied ethnicities and creeds came. There was much hugging, crying, and flag-waving. Governor Jesse Ventura expressed the feelings of all Minnesotans in attendance. "We can all be proud to be Minnesotans and Americans today," he said.

The Capitol is also a symbol of authority. It stands for the sovereign state of Minnesota. Consequently, it is the place where many dramas of democracy have played out over the course of a century. The governor and the elected officials who work there have the weighty responsibility of representing the interests of a diverse Minnesota. Making everyone happy is an impossible task. The fifty steps that lead to the front doors have often become an

elevated stage for dramatic public demonstrations meant to garner attention for causes. The rotunda has also seen its share of rallies and protests. Many of the views expressed at the Capitol by Minnesota's citizenry are not popular with every audience, but democracy gives the freedom to speak one's mind.

Nearly twenty thousand overall-clad farmers stormed the corridors and galleries and amassed on the front steps of the Capitol on March 22, 1933. The Great Depression had set in, and they were in dire need. The farmers demanded moratoriums on the foreclosures and evictions that were taking away their

A fan celebrates the Minnesota Twins' second World Series win at a parade in October 1991.

farms. They wanted lower interest rates for themselves and higher taxes for chain stores and oleomargarine, a competitor of Minnesota's butter. The legislature had been in session since January 1, and no decisions had been made about relief. Governor Floyd B. Olson blamed the lollygagging Senate and the "reactionary conservatives" in the upper House. Mixed with the farmers' pleas for debt and tax relief were threats of retaliation against state legislators. "Much worse than the Boston Tea Party will happen unless farmers are given relief from tax and debt burdens," warned one of their spokesmen. "If something

is not done in the next two years you will see plenty of bloodshed," another spokesman added. They were desperate.

Half a century later, during what was called the toughest times for agriculture since the 1930s, more than ten thousand farmers marched on the State Capitol, many wearing snowmobile suits to protect them from the bitter January cold. It was 1985, and the farmers were again asking for moratoriums on foreclosures and debt relief. The 1980s had not been kind to rural America. One speaker at Minnesota's Capitol prompted a roar from the

Desperate Minnesota farmers dragged a starving cow and horse up the stairs of the State Capitol to dramatize their demands for governmental relief in 1935.

Minnesotans liked "Ike," as shown by a 1952 campaign blimp sporting Dwight D. Eisenhower's nickname.

crowd on the steps when she quipped, "If the government can afford billions for star wars in space, then it can afford money for food here on earth!" The demonstrators needed to foster pubic awareness in order to sway the lawmakers. Nineteen eighty-five was the year that country-western singer Willie Nelson and other celebrities used the media to this end when they organized the first "Farm Aid" concert to draw attention to the plight of America's farmers. At the Minnesota Capitol, farmers and their families carried their protest signs to the front steps. "If you eat, you need us," one of the signs read. The farmers had big banners and loudspeakers that day, and the television cameras were whirring.

Demonstrating at the Capitol is about grabbing attention. Sometimes this can be done with words, and sometimes visuals are more powerful. A recent protester of Minnesota's gun law took to the Capitol with a sign reading, "Conceal and carry is a turkey of a law!" He was dressed in a turkey costume.

Minnesota's attorney general Hubert H. "Skip" Humphrey III, son of Minnesota statesman and U.S. vice president Hubert H. Humphrey II, explains citizenship to Girl Scouts, ca. 1980.

TOURS AND PORTRAITS

People also come to Minnesota's Capitol on pleasant terms. The Capitol tour is a rite of passage for the state's schoolchildren, and it is equally popular with adults. Visitors learn about the history of the building and what the murals represent. They marvel at the size of the massive chandelier hanging high in the rotunda and learn that it is lowered all the way to the first floor on a heavy chain for cleaning—although not very often! They see the House Chamber from the second-level viewing gallery, and venture up the cantilevered staircase at the northeast corner of the rotunda.

Weather permitting, the lucky visitor gets to go out onto the Capitol's roof and stand next to the golden quadriga.

The portraits that line some walls of the first floor and basement were never a highlight of the Capitol tour. Upstairs, tucked away in a dim hall, are the painted head-and-shoulders likenesses of the governors who served Minnesota through the turn of the nineteenth century. Notable men with notable names such as Henry H. Sibley and John S. Pillsbury stare out at the visitor from the stately canvases bordered by gilded frames. The stars, gophers, and lady's slippers that decorate the frame of John Johnson's portrait are special highlights.

Things liven up a bit on the lower level. Some of Minnesota's twentieth-century governors added personal touches to their portraits. The tradition has each outgoing governor commission an artist to paint his official portrait to hang in the Capitol. In his portrait, a dapper, slick-haired Floyd B. Olson holds a microphone that makes him look like an old-time radio announcer.

Rudy Perpich included his wife, Lola, in his portrait. Arne Carlson chose to do away with

stuffy formal attire for his portrait and instead donned a University of Minnesota letter jacket and a pair of khaki pants.

There was some concern in 2003, but mostly amused anticipation, when Governor Jesse Ventura chose his former tag-team wrestling partner to paint his official portrait. "What if the picture shows him wearing a feather boa?" countless Minnesotans asked in mock alarm. Governor Ventura was a former pro wrestler and Hollywood action star turned Brooklyn Park mayor who literally "shocked the world" when he won the 1998 gubernatorial election in Minnesota on a third-party

Floyd B. Olson chose to pose with a microphone.

Rudy Perpich's portrait includes his wife, Lola.

ticket. During his wrestling days he was known for his flamboyant style. During his four years as Minnesota's chief executive he was known for bucking the system. Who knew what he would do next?

Arne Carlson wanted a more casual portrait.

The *St. Paul Pioneer Press* commissioned local artists to create their own versions of Ventura's gubernatorial portrait. Results ranged from traditional ceramic tile mosaics to digital animation. There were plenty of feather boas in the lot. One artist alluded to Ventura's effort to legalize fireworks in Minnesota by creating a flashy, fluorescent likeness of the governor as

a fireworks package. Another paid homage to the governor's own action figure that showed up in his television advertisements during the 1998 election. Four years had given the artists plenty of media moments to work with.

Governor Ventura's official portrait was unveiled in November 2003. The artist, Steve Cepello, also known as "Steve Strong" or the "California Terminator" during his wrestling days with Ventura, called the picture a "dignified, loving portrait of a statesman." Many were surprised that the portrait of the untraditional governor was fairly traditional. The painting sets Ventura against a dark, menacing sky. The Capitol, a light-rail train, a golf hole, and the Minneapolis skyline are in the background. The governor's dark blue suit sets off his American flag tie and Navy Seal pins. In one hand he holds a lighted cigar. His other hand rests on a miniature version of Auguste Rodin's *The Thinker*, a reference to the 1998 television ad campaign in which Ventura posed as the famous sculpture, declaring himself no longer "Jesse the Body," but "Jesse the Mind." Indeed, his portrait shows him gazing into the distance, deep in thought.

Now when visitors tour the Capitol, they make a beeline for the governors' portraits in the basement. Some are interested in finding the "hidden symbolism" they had heard was present in the Ventura portrait. Others just want to see if it looks like the guy they knew from TV.

In his day, Governor John Johnson was equally famous with Minnesotans, but for different reasons. He was an avid baseball fan, known to umpire Little League games in his hometown of St. Peter, Minnesota, where he had worked as a newspaper editor. He was elected to the State Senate in 1898 on a Democratic ticket, a remarkable achievement at a time when Minnesota was overwhelmingly Republican. Abundantly charming, Johnson was popular with the citizens who elected him to the governor's office in 1904, 1906, and 1908. And his ability to work with both parties resulted in important reform legislation.

Governor Johnson began his third term in precarious health. Following a surgery, he died unexpectedly in 1909. He was the first of Minnesota's governors to die while in office, and the first to lie in state in the Capitol rotunda. Minnesotans were grief-stricken. A committee was set up to seek donations for a fitting monument to their idol. No one was allowed to submit more than one dollar. The $25,000 raised for the memorial was a testament to his popularity.

In October 1912, thousands of Minnesotans gathered in front of the Capitol. They were there for the unveiling and dedication of the John Johnson memorial statue, which stands on a granite pedestal at the base of the Capitol steps. Four workers of Minnesota industry—a farmer, an ironworker, a timber cruiser, and a miner—surround the tall, bronze likeness of the late governor. The sculpture was another in a series of firsts for John Johnson. It was the first of many memorials to be placed on the Capitol grounds.

Governor John A. Johnson memorial cigars were issued a year after his sudden death in office in 1909.

A statue memorializes Governor John Johnson in front of the Capitol.

Elmer L. Andersen, who served as Minnesota's thirtieth governor from 1961 to 1963, lies in state in the Capitol rotunda. He died November 15, 2004, at the age of ninety-five.

Return of the Rathskeller

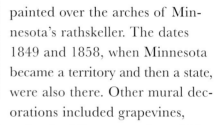

Where might a weary, parched legislator of 1905 go when not in session? Why, the rathskeller, of course! Architect Cass Gilbert gave Minnesota's State Capitol its own underground German-themed beer hall. There the Minnesotan lawmaker could indulge in a pint or two and a bite to eat before returning to work. Rathskeller is the name for below-street-level beer saloons that originated in German town halls. The theme suited the basement space available for a restaurant. Since Germans were the largest immigrant population in Minnesota in 1905, it also made sense to honor their heritage somewhere in the new Capitol.

Gilbert and Elmer Garnsey, the lead decorator, collaborated on the interior design of the rathskeller. Traditionally, the walls of nineteenth-century rathskellers were decorated with German sayings. "Enjoy a glass after a duty well performed," "Better be tipsy than feverish," and "If you have time, don't wait for another time" are some examples of the twenty-nine clever aphorisms painted over the arches of Minnesota's rathskeller. The dates 1849 and 1858, when Minnesota became a territory and then a state, were also there. Other mural decorations included grapevines, flowers, Americanized German eagles, rabbits, and frolicking squirrels that looked like they had jumped straight out of an old German storybook—a refreshing contrast to the high-hat allegorical figures on the Capitol's upper floors.

Public sentiment during World War I dealt harshly with Minnesota's rathskeller. Lobbying by people looking to control alcohol consumption, aided and abetted by others who saw Germans as enemies, led to an order by Governor J. A. A. Burnquist to have the German phrases painted over. In 1930, "cleaned up" versions of the mottoes were repainted on the walls, but over the years the German flavor of the restaurant remained under multiple coats of paint. Restoring the rathskeller was one part of the larger State Capitol restoration campaign that was launched in the mid-1980s.

Research efforts and skilled restoration artists returned Gilbert's building to its original splendor. A perennially leaky roof was repaired. Conservators removed decades of grime from Senate murals in 1988. Original furniture and carpet were restored or re-created. After designs painstakingly recovered from under years of paint layers offered clues about what the original murals looked like. Most of the murals were repainted on a fresh layer of plaster. Patches of the original murals were left in places so visitors can compare the restored art

Part of the Capitol restoration efforts was a cleanup of the rathskeller.

eighty-eight years of exposure to the elements had taken its toll on the golden quadriga, a large crane hoisted the sculpture from its place on the roof in 1994. It was trucked away, restored, regilded, and repositioned in 1995.

Restoration of the basement rathskeller began in 1994. Photographs and remnants of the against the old. The tables, chairs, and light fixtures were reproduced to match the designs of 1905. Now, legislators, staff, and visitors to the Capitol can again enjoy breakfast or lunch in the Rathskeller Café, as the building's architect envisioned it a century ago. Although beer is no longer on the menu, the subterranean spot still feels authentic.

A restored Rathskeller Café boasts Americanized German eagles on its ceiling.

This image of the Cathedral of St. Paul was drawn by its French architect, Emmanuel L. Masqueray.

chapter six

Minnesota on the Mall

JUNE 1905 was a busy month for Archbishop John Ireland of St. Paul. As the former chaplain of the Fifth Minnesota Regiment, he captivated and inspired the Flag Day crowds gathered on the steps of the new Capitol with his eloquent tribute to American patriotism.

But his mind that month was also on St. Paul's other hill. The French architect Emmanuel L. Masqueray had submitted his first sketches for the new Catholic cathedral to be built to the southwest of the Capitol, on St. Anthony Hill. The overcrowding that was the death knell for Minnesota's second Capitol building on Tenth and Cedar had also beset the St. Peter Street cathedral. The brimming congregation during Holy Week in 1904 had prompted Archbishop Ireland to launch a building campaign. His majestic Cathedral of St. Paul would share the city skyline with Cass Gilbert's monument to the state and the ever-taller commercial buildings rising in downtown.

Ireland's vision for the Cathedral of St. Paul shared many of the goals of the State Capitol planners. It was to be a shining structure that would reflect a strong and unified community

grown from the diverse immigrant groups that made Minnesota their home. To crown St. Anthony Hill, Masqueray designed a domed, Renaissance-style cathedral based on St. Peter's

Born in Ireland and educated for the priesthood in France, John Ireland was Minnesota's first archbishop.

in Rome. The Capitol was receiving its finishing touches when ground was broken for this grand edifice in 1906. On March 28, 1915, Palm Sunday, Archbishop Ireland celebrated the first Mass in the new cathedral.

THE CAPITOL APPROACH

The building campaign and location of the cathedral may have been advanced by talk of a broad parkway approach leading to the State Capitol. The rules of the 1895 Minnesota State Capitol design competition clearly stated that architects were not to include any type of landscaping around the building in their designs. After gaining the commission, however, Cass Gilbert lobbied hard for support of

a beautiful "yard" for the Capitol. He imagined broad boulevards and open vistas like those constructed in Paris during the nineteenth century. He believed that St. Paul could rival the grandest of European cities.

The National Mall in Washington, D.C., the two-mile-long boulevard that extends from the federal Capitol to the Lincoln Memorial, was being tidied up in 1902. During the nineteenth century, the Mall, as it is called, was essentially a long, muddy paddock used for temporary markets and exotic animal exhibits. The early-twentieth-century sprucing up transformed the Mall into a lush, green park with trees, museums, monuments, and

This aerial view of the Capitol approach area, ca. 1957, shows Cass Gilbert's triaxial design. The Capitol looks straight up the axis on the left to the Cathedral of St. Paul.

The Peace Officers Memorial by Fred Richter remembers Minnesota law enforcement officers.

memorials. Gilbert wanted the same for St. Paul. A grand approach would set off Minnesota's hilltop Capitol and beautify the surrounding area, which consisted mostly of deteriorating neighborhoods. The greenery would be a refuge from the ugliness of the industry and commerce.

Gilbert's plan was a grand one: three main axes would radiate south from the Capitol like a fan, one straight up St. Anthony Hill to the future site of the Cathedral of St. Paul. The others would open the views from the downtown business district and Seven Corners. Gilbert envisioned a tall war memorial in a park at the halfway point of the central axis.

Gilbert's dream for a grand Capitol approach languished for lack of funds, however. It was not until after World War II that a Capitol approach would be constructed in St. Paul. The state of Minnesota and the city of St. Paul first acquired fifty-three acres south of the Capitol building, and demolition of buildings on the land began in 1949. By 1953, the St. Paul Winter Carnival parade traveled from Summit Avenue at the Cathedral through the developing Capitol approach area. That same year, construction began on the Veterans' Service Building, a modern structure at the end of Minnesota's Capitol Mall. The Centennial Office Building and the Transportation Building would follow.

In 1957, Minnesotans plucky enough to try the Winter Carnival toboggan slide followed the path of the Cedar Avenue arm of the new Capitol approach. The approach did not end up being as grandiose as Cass Gilbert had planned. The final design did retain his original triaxial pattern, however. When it was completed, it was a significant improvement over what the site had been.

The Capitol approach area designers of the 1940s and 1950s had to work around a few beloved statues already in place on the Capitol grounds. The statue of Governor John A. Johnson that had been installed at the base of the Capitol steps in 1912 was the first of many monuments and memorials outside of the Capitol. In 1928 Johnson's predecessor in office, Governor Knute Nelson, joined him at the end of the steps. Three years later, Christopher Columbus arrived.

WITH ETHNIC PRIDE

Almost twenty-five thousand Italians, one local newspaper reported, gathered in the park in front of the Minnesota Historical Society

Hundreds of citizens attended the dedication of the Governor John Johnson memorial statue in 1912.

The Governor Knute Nelson Memorial by John K. Daniels was erected in 1928. Born in Norway, Nelson was the first Scandinavian to be elected governor of Minnesota.

With Ethnic Pride (**Christopher Columbus**), **sculpted by Italian-American Carlo Brioschi, was installed in 1931.**

Lionizing Columbus and other historical figures was common during the 1920s, 1930s, and 1940s. Faced with all the newness of modern life, then the depression, and then World War II, many Americans sought refuge in the past. Knowing one's roots somehow made things a bit more bearable. Moreover, the great wave of European immigration into U.S. cities during the 1910s brought many Italians to America and to Minnesota.

Then in 1924, the U.S. government passed an Immigration Act that curtailed the flood of immigration from southern and eastern Europe. People from these areas already living in the United States bristled because the law characterized them as "undesirables." The title of the Columbus statue—*With Ethnic Pride*—tells us that Minnesota's Italian community was working in 1931 to foster a more positive view of their heritage.

The Columbus dedication ceremony was a big deal. A procession of marching bands, dignitaries, children waving Italian flags, and several groups of Italian-Americans from all over Minnesota wound through the streets of downtown St. Paul from Union Depot to the Capitol. Fifteen men representing the United States, Italy, and Minnesota gave speeches. Via a radio hook-up with Washington, D.C., the attorney general of the United States spoke to the crowd in St. Paul. "Minnesotans should be proud to have the countrymen of Christopher Columbus in their midst," he told them. A telegram from President Herbert Hoover praised the explorer: "In him action matched

building (now the Judicial Center) at the southeastern corner of the Capitol on Columbus Day, October 12, 1931. They were celebrating the dedication of a memorial statue to Christopher Columbus. Its title is *With Ethnic Pride*, an appropriate name for a statue paid for by Minnesota's Italian-Americans and sculpted by an Italian immigrant, Carlo Brioschi.

imagination and courage conquered all obstacles." These were poignant and comforting words for the depression-era crowd.

AMERIGO, THE OTHER BRIOSCHI

Amerigo Brioschi, son of Carlo Brioschi, was also a sculptor. His work at the Minnesota State Capitol includes a bronze statue of Governor Floyd B. Olson, which is located opposite Carlo's Columbus statue on the west side of the Capitol grounds, and a bronze tablet in the rotunda. But the mural Amerigo and his father designed for the House of Representatives is more memorable. Unlike the murals in the other chambers, *Minnesota, Spirit of Government* is a painting *and* a sculpture. It is a three-dimensional plaster sculpture set against a painted background.

The Brioschi mural is located directly above the speaker's desk and a portrait of Abraham Lincoln. The State Emergency Relief Administration, a depression-era program that aided Minnesotans who might otherwise have had a hard time finding work in the desperate economy, commissioned the mural. When installed in 1938, it walled off a public viewing gallery to make more office space.

The House of Representatives faces *Minnesota, Spirit of Government* by Carlo and Amerigo Brioschi.

Minnesota, Spirit of Government is similar to the two murals painted by Edwin Blashfield for the Senate Chamber in that it is a mix of idealized figures and real Minnesota history. In the middle, "Minnesota" is a goddesslike figure who stands on a pedestal emblazoned with the state seal. She represents the spirit of good government. The other figures—two Native Americans, a trapper, and a French voyageur—stand amid bountiful piles of fruit and vegetables. The mural's painted caption, "The Trail of the Pioneer Bore the Footprints of Liberty," connects the history of Minnesota with the governmental function of the room.

THE VIKING RIVAL

On the west side of the Capitol grounds, bordered by University and Constitution Avenues, stands a statue of Christopher Columbus's rival in exploration—Leif Erikson, the Viking explorer many believe to be the first European to have reached America, almost five hundred years before Columbus. Minnesota's Norwegian-American community financed this statue.

There was some concern in 1949, the year of Minnesota's territorial centennial, that the Leif Erikson statue was in jeopardy. The worry was fueled by the ongoing crusade of Johan Andreas Holvik, a Concordia College Norwegian professor who devoted much of his career to discrediting the Kensington runestone. The authenticity of the stone, a rock slab bearing a carved runic inscription telling a story of Norwegian exploration to Minnesota in 1362, was in doubt from the day it was "discovered" in 1898 by a Swedish immigrant on his farm

near Kensington, Minnesota. The efforts of some to validate the claims of early exploration in Minnesota, and the resolve of others to discredit those claims, led to an ongoing public debate that finally came to a boil in 1949.

Holvik had spent years building his case against the Kensington runestone. Local Scandinavian-American pride, however, made his position somewhat unpopular. Then in August 1949, a *Minneapolis Tribune* reporter published a pointed article based on Holvik's evidence. This most recent public assertion that the stone was a hoax fell at a bad time for the Minnesota Leif Erikson Monument Association, which was in the middle of a fundraising drive for its sculpture for the Capitol. The negative press about the stone would discourage donations, complained R. J. Meland, secretary of the association. His worrying was for naught, however. The thirteen-foot bronze statue of the Viking explorer was erected as planned and unveiled on Leif Erikson Day, October 9, 1949, in front of a crowd numbering about three thousand.

JOHN KARL DANIELS

The sculptor of the Leif Erikson statue was John Karl Daniels. Following the triumph of his Minnesota State Capitol butter sculpture for the 1901 Pan-American Exposition in Buffalo, New York, Daniels became one of the most accomplished sculptors in Minnesota. His other well-known works include the Leif Erikson statue in Duluth, the three terra-cotta millers on the Washburn-Crosby Milling Company building (now the Washburn Lofts)

Minnesota's Norwegian-American community paid for this imposing sculpture of Leif Erikson by John K. Daniels. It was unveiled before a crowd of three thousand citizens who gathered for the occasion on Leif Erikson Day, October 9, 1949.

John K. Daniels works on a model of his Leif Erikson sculpture in his studio in 1949.

in downtown Minneapolis, the eagles on Washburn Tower, and the Allianz Life Insurance Building buffalo in Minneapolis. In 1884 at the age of ten, Daniels had moved with his family from Norway to St. Paul, where he learned sculpting at the Manual Training High School. His studio was a converted icehouse on LaSalle Avenue in Minneapolis. He worked there until he died at age 103 in 1978.

Daniels's legacy at the Capitol includes his bronzes of two Civil War officers, General John B. Sanborn and Colonel Alexander Wilkinson, which occupy tall niches on the second level of the rotunda. His bust of Ignatius Donnelly, a colorful nineteenth-century figure in Minnesota and national politics, is on the

first level. In 1928 Daniels honored Republican governor Knute Nelson, a fellow Norwegian-American. Paired with the statue of Governor John Johnson, a Democrat, the tall sculpture of Nelson makes for a bipartisan frame for the Capitol steps. Nelson was the first governor of Minnesota from Norway. A Viking ship is carved into the granite pedestal on which his statue stands. Below him and to his right, figures of a woman and a child represent his experience as an immigrant; he and his mother came to America in 1849. Nelson served with the Wisconsin Volunteer Infantry during the Civil War, hence the figure of a soldier on the other side of the base. In 1871 Nelson came to Minnesota, where he served in the State Senate and as governor from 1893 to 1895.

For nearly two years, from July 1954 until June 1956, Daniels chipped away at an eight-ton block of Vermont marble inside a small wood and tarpaper shed on the Capitol grounds. The result of the octogenarian's artistic zeal was *Earthbound*, a classical-looking male figure emerging from a rough-hewn block of stone. According to Daniels, the statue symbolizes "mankind's everlasting struggle for freedom." Daniels had gone allegorical late in his career! *Earthbound* stands on one side of the stairs of the Veterans Administration Building. On the other side of the steps is a copy of America's Liberty Bell, cast in France and paid for by American metal corporations.

RECENT MEMORIALS

Minnesota veterans who fought in the wars of the nineteenth century are memorialized in the

Capitol rotunda and the Governor's Reception Room. Outside, on the Capitol Mall, Minnesota veterans of modern wars are remembered with four memorials.

The Civil War and Spanish-American War veterans who returned to St. Paul to escort their battle flags from the old Capitol to the new statehouse in 1905, and those who demanded that their battles be commemorated with "real" pictures and lifelike bronze statues, did so with purpose. They were proud of their service, and they wanted to honor their comrades who had been lost in war. The Civil War veterans wanted a place at the Capitol where they would be remembered. Each modern war memorial on the Mall, though very different from a painting or a tattered flag, serves the same purpose for Minnesotan veterans. The artistic styles have changed, but the meaning remains the same.

Other memorials on the Capitol Mall are dedicated to individual Minnesotans. *The Boy and the Man,* a bronze statue commemorating Charles Lindbergh, the first person to fly solo and non-stop across the Atlantic, was dedicated in 1985. Two bronze figures represent a boy's dream of flying and the accomplished aviator the boy became. Though Lindbergh was born in Detroit, Michigan, he is considered a native son because he grew up near Little Falls, Minnesota. Two other castings of this sculpture exist. One is located at the San Diego International Airport and the other at Le Bourget Field in Paris.

Decidedly different in style, the Roy Wilkins Memorial, dedicated in 1995, is located near

Lindbergh's statue. St. Paulite Roy Wilkins was a leader in the American civil-rights movement of the 1950s and 1960s. His memorial consists of a series of spiraling copper pyramids and obelisks that represent a visual conception of breaking the barriers of racial segregation.

Earthbound, **by John K. Daniels, was installed on the Capitol Mall in 1956.**

A placid place for reflection, the Minnesota Vietnam Veterans Memorial, *Lakefront DMZ,* by Nina Akerberg, Jake Castillo, Rick Laffin, and Stanton Sears, was dedicated in 1982.

The most recent addition to the State Capitol Mall is the Woman's Suffrage Memorial, the *Garden of Time.* Dedicated in 2000, it includes a trellis with the names of twenty-five Minnesota suffragists and quotes from suffrage leaders. A bronze timeline tells the story of the women's movement in America leading up to the ratification of the Nineteenth Amendment in 1920, which granted women the vote. Recently, the plantings were changed because of compatibility problems with the soil, but the original idea called for yellow daffodils to bloom in the gardens during the spring. Yellow was the color linked with the suffrage movement. Native woodland and prairie flowers would bloom for the rest of the season.

The Women's Suffrage Memorial was designed to be a living history lesson. In truth, the entire Capitol approach is a living lesson in history. It is an evolving record of significant social and political moments for Minnesotans. From popular governors to hometown heroes, Minnesotans who made a difference are remembered there.

The Minnesota State Capitol building is a history lesson too. Through its classical columns, marble surfaces, golden quadriga, high-class murals, battle flags, bronze gophers, and carved lady's slippers, it tells the story of what was important to Minnesotans a century ago. Some of what was important then—demonstrating the stability of a young state and showing the

The cut-out silhouette of a soldier in the Minnesota Korean War Memorial, by sculptor Art Norby and landscape architects Bob Kost and Dean Olson, represents missing-in-action soldiers. Names of the seven hundred Minnesotans who died in the conflict are engraved on stone markers behind the sculpture.

East that the West was equally civilized—does not seem as necessary or relevant in the Internet age. But as a symbol of democratic government and a unifying touchstone for Minnesotans, the building is just as meaningful as ever. Moreover, as they did when the building was completed in 1905, Minnesotans still look to their Capitol as a showplace, a monument to the state and its people, one constant in an era of hastening transformation and an enduring, beautiful "marble pile" on the hill.

The Minnesotans who gathered on an empty plot of land on top of Wabasha Hill in the spring of 1896 for the groundbreaking ceremony for their new Capitol were there for a reason. They wanted to be able to tell the story in years to come of how they were there when it all began. They knew that something great was about to take shape. Nine years later, Minnesota's Capitol was complete, and they were right—it *was* magnificent. Today, after weathering a century, it is just as grand. But the people standing on the hill knew already that it would be. Any building that represented the great state of Minnesota could be nothing less. "Hip, hip, hurrah!" they cheered as they giddily pitched the first shovels full of dirt. And now, in 2005, we can shout gladly, "And here's to a hundred years more!"

The Roy Wilkins Memorial by sculptor Curtis Patterson was dedicated on the Capitol Mall in 1995. Wilkins's lifelong work with the NAACP (National Association for the Advancement of Colored People) led to the Civil Rights Acts of 1957, 1960, and 1964, and the Voting Rights Act of 1965.

The Charles Lindbergh Memorial by Paul Granlund is a life-size bronze titled *The Boy and the Man*. The boy dreams of flying and the man realizes that dream. Raised on a farm near Little Falls, Minnesota, Lindbergh was the first person to fly solo and non-stop across the Atlantic Ocean in May 1927.

Capitol Activities

Chapter One

LETTERS HOME: The year is 1850. You are a settler arriving in Minnesota Territory. Write a letter to your family or friends about life on the frontier. What was the main reason you immigrated to Minnesota? How did you travel? Where have you made your home? How will you make a living? What do you think of your new environment? How are things in Minnesota different from where you came?

ADVERTISING MINNESOTA: Be a booster! Make an ad for Minnesota to attract new settlement in 1858, Minnesota's first year of statehood. What are your "selling points"? How will you catch people's attention? Where will your ad circulate?

HOMETOWN HISTORY: Do you know your local history? Research the founding and settlement of your town. Who arrived first? When and from where did they come? Why did they come? What did they do once they arrived?

Chapter Two

DESIGN A CAPITOL: How would *you* design Minnesota's Capitol? In your opinion, what is an appropriate style to represent your state in 2005? What would you change? What would stay the same? Decorate your building with symbols that might appeal to a broad range of Minnesotans. Give reasons for your choices, and be bold. Cass Gilbert was!

CAPITOL DRAMA: Make reader theater! Write, direct, and act in a play about how Minnesota's Capitol came into being. Who will be your main characters? What roles did they play in the process?

COMPARING CAPITOLS: Research other state capitols being built around the same time as Minnesota's. What do they look like? How are they similar to the Capitol in St. Paul? How are they different? Here is a Web site at which to start your research: **www.cupola.com/html/bldgstru/statecap/slide/captour.html**

Chapter Three

TIME TRAVELER: The Capitol is open! You are a reporter from the year 2005. You travel back in time one hundred years to January 2, 1905, and become one of the first Minnesotans to view the Capitol on opening day. Upon your return to 2005 you must write a news broadcast for television. What do you have to say about the event? What are your first impressions of the building? What do you see? Include interview testimonials from several other Minnesotans who were there. Who are these people and what did they think of their visit? If you have recording equipment, videotape your broadcast and show it to your class.

MAKE A MURAL: Using a large roll of paper, design and produce a mural that commemorates and celebrates an important period or event in the history of Minnesota or your town. What story will you tell? Which historical figures will you include or exclude? What is the best way to visualize your story—with one big image, as in Minnesota's Senate Chamber, or with a series of images, as in the rotunda? And make your art public! When you are finished, hang your mural in your classroom or somewhere else in your school.

NEWS AROUND THE WORLD: What else was happening in the United States and in the world in the year the Minnesota State Capitol was completed? Use library sources and the Internet to find out. Make a list of important people, events, and popular entertainments of 1905.

Chapter Four

CIVIL WAR REPORTERS: Find a partner to share this activity with you. One of you will be a newspaper reporter from the North assigned to cover the Battle of Gettysburg in 1863. The other will be a reporter from the South assigned to cover the battle. Each of you will write articles for your papers about what happened at Gettysburg. Use library and Internet resources for your research. If possible, use microfilm resources at your library to read period newspaper accounts of the battle.

MINNESOTA'S NATIVE AMERICANS: Use library and Internet resources to learn more about the history and culture of Native Americans in Minnesota. Create a class presentation with PowerPoint or poster boards that includes words and images. Write the text yourself. Find images from Web sites or scan or photocopy them from books or other resources.

Chapter Five

STATE OF THE STATE: Find out more about state government in Minnesota. What is the role of each branch of government? Who is the current gov-ernor? How many senators serve Minnesota? How many representatives? How many Supreme Court justices does Minnesota have? How long are their terms? What do they do?

GOVERNORS' BIOGRAPHIES: Know your Minnesota governors! How many have there been since Minnesota became a state? Choose two governors and research and write short biographies for them. Which political parties did they belong to? When did they serve? Were there any unusual political challenges they had to face while in office? What political issues were they associated with?

Chapter Six

CREATE A MONUMENT: You have been chosen to research and design a new monument for the Capitol grounds to commemorate one Minnesotan or a group of Minnesotans who have made history. Divide the class into "civic committees" of four students each. Each group will propose an idea for the new memorial. Your proposals will include a biographical statement about the person or group you want to memorialize, your reasons for wanting to commemorate this person or group, and a scale model of your memorial. Decide how you can fairly split these tasks among your committee members. When you are finished, present your proposals to the rest of the class. Then hold a democratic vote that will decide which memorial will be built at the Minnesota State Capitol.

MONUMENTAL RESEARCH: Research the public memorials in your town. Who or what is commemorated? When were the monuments made or installed? Who paid for them?

BIBLIOGRAPHY

"After the attack," *Star Tribune* (September 17, 2001).

Blodgett, Geoffrey. *Cass Gilbert: The Early Years.* St. Paul: Minnesota Historical Society Press, 2001.

Cass Gilbert papers, Minnesota Historical Society manuscript collection, St. Paul.

Christen, Barbara S., and Steven Flanders, eds. *Cass Gilbert, Life and Work: Architect of the Public Domain.* New York and London: W. W. Norton and Company, 2001.

Coffmann, Jack B., and Bill Salisbury. "Farmers cry out for aid to survive 'toughest times,'" *St. Paul Pioneer Press and Dispatch* (January 29, 1985).

"Columbus statue, facing homeland, noted as shrine," *St. Paul Pioneer Press* (October 13, 1931).

Conforti, Michael, ed. *Minnesota 1900: Art and Life on the Upper Mississippi, 1890–1915.* Newark: University of Delaware Press in association with the Minneapolis Institute of Arts, 1994.

"Farmers flay Senate as they demand relief," *St. Paul Pioneer Press* (March 23, 1933).

Ferguson, Franklin T. "The Cathedral of St. Paul," *Minnesota History* (Winter 1964): 153–62.

"5000 pay tribute to explorer Leif Erickson at unveiling of statue on Capitol grounds," *St. Paul Pioneer Press* (October 10, 1949).

"Flags of two wars now in Capitol," *Minneapolis Journal* (June 14, 1905).

Gauthier, Julie C. *The Minnesota Capitol: Official Guide and History.* St. Paul: Pioneer Press, 1907.

Gilbert, Cass, and Julia Finch Gilbert, ed. *Reminisces and Addresses.* New York: Scribner Press, 1935.

Goodsell, Charles T. *The American Statehouse: Interpreting Democracy's Temples.* Lawrence, Kansas: University of Kansas Press, 2001.

Hauck, Eldon. *American Capitols: An Encyclopedia of the State, National, and Territorial Edifices of the United States.* Jefferson, North Carolina: McFarland and Company, 1991.

Heilbrun, Margaret. *Inventing the Skyline: The Architecture of Cass Gilbert.* New York: Columbia University Press, 2000.

Hill, Patrick M. "The 28th Virginia Regiment's Flag in Minnesota," *Minnesota History* (Summer 2000): 58–73.

Hitchcock, Henry-Russell, and William Seale. *Temples of Democracy: The State Capitols of the USA.* New York and London: Harcourt Brace Jovanovich, 1976.

Irish, Sharon. *Cass Gilbert, Architect: Modern Traditionalist.* New York: Monacelli Press, 1999.

Irish, Sharon. "West Hails East: Cass Gilbert in Minnesota," *Minnesota History* (Spring 1993): 196–207.

"John A. Johnson made governor of Minnesota," *Minneapolis Tribune* (January 5, 1905).

John Karl Daniel papers, Hennepin History Museum manuscript collection, Minneapolis.

Larson, Paul Clifford. *Cass Gilbert Abroad: The Young Architect's European Tour.* Afton, Minnesota: Afton Historical Society Press, 2002.

Lass, William E. *Minnesota: A History,* 2nd ed. New York and London: W. W. Norton and Company, 1998 (1977).

"Leif Erikson Statue Unveiled," *Minneapolis Morning Tribune* (October 10, 1949).

Marling, Karal Ann. *Old Glory: Unfurling History.* Charlestown, Massachusetts: Bunker Hill Publishing in association with the Library of Congress, 2005.

Marling, Karal Ann. *Blue Ribbon: A Social and Pictorial History of the Minnesota State Fair.* St. Paul: Minnesota Historical Society Press, 1990.

Marling, Karal Ann. "She Brought Forth Butter in a Lordly Dish: The Origins of Minnesota Butter Sculpture," *Minnesota History* (Summer 1987): 218–28.

"Many visitors are attracted to new Capitol," *St. Paul Pioneer Press* (January 3, 1905).

Minnesota Board of Managers. "The Bread and Butter State." Report of the Minnesota Board of Managers for the Pan-American Exposition at Buffalo, New York, May 1 to November 1, 1901. St. Paul: Pioneer Press Company, 1902.

"Minnesota's new Capitol is most beautiful in country," *Minneapolis Tribune* (January 8, 1905).

"New Capitol ablaze," *Minneapolis Tribune* (January 3, 1905).

"New Capitol a dazzling gem," *St. Paul Pioneer Press* (January 3, 1905).

The North-Western Line, "The Dairy Interests of Minnesota, Minnesota's Capitol in Butter" (St. Paul, 1901).

O'Connor, Debra, and Mara H. Gottfried. "A state of strength," *St. Paul Pioneer Press and Dispatch* (September 17, 2001).

O'Sullivan, Thomas. *Northstar Statehouse: An Armchair Guide to the Minnesota State Capitol.* St. Paul: Pogo Press, 1994.

Patteson, Lewis, and Donald Giese. "War Protesters Here March for Peace," *St. Paul Pioneer Press* (May 10, 1970).

Report of Capitol Approaches Commission to the Council of the City of St. Paul (St. Paul: Capitol Approaches Commission, 1906).

Ruggiero, Francis Pio. *State Capitols: Temples of Sovereignty.* Milford, Pennsylvania: Excelsior, 2002.

Salisbury, Bill. "Minnesota farm tax relief bills turn into hot potatoes in House," *St. Paul Pioneer Press and Dispatch* (January 29, 1985).

"Seabury starts it," *Minneapolis Journal* (May 6, 1896).

Sprunger, David; Susap, Peter; and Weixel, Elizabeth. *J. A. Holvik and the Kensington Runestone: A Study in Ethnic, Religious, and Community Identity.* http://www.cord.edu/dept/teachatcord/centennial/Sprunger1997.htm

Thompson, Neil B. *Minnesota's State Capitol: The Art and Politics of a Public Building.* St. Paul: Minnesota Historical Society, 1974.

Thompson, Neil B. "A Half Century of Capitol Conflict: How St. Paul Kept the Seat of Government," *Minnesota History* (Fall 1973): pp. 238–54.

"Transfer of the historic battle flags," *Minneapolis Journal* (June 13, 1905).

Van Hook, Bailey. *The Virgin and the Dynamo: Public Murals in American Architecture, 1893–1917.* Athens, Ohio: Ohio University Press, 2003.

Wilson, Richard D., et al. *American Renaissance, 1876–1917.* Brooklyn, New York: Brooklyn Museum, 1979.

http://www.caapb.state.mn.us/ (accessed July 19, 2004).

ILLUSTRATION CREDITS

B. F. FORSTER, St. Paul, Minnesota
The Capitol of Minnesota, 1905: **p. 24,** State Capitol board of commissioners, photograph by Alfred Zimmerman; **p. 29,** Alexander Ramsey and silver trowel; **p. 37,** Capitol under construction; **p. 45,** electric light standard; **p. 60,** *Prudence*, sculpture by Daniel Chester French, ca. 1900; **p. 79,** flag case.

JORGE ZEGARRA LEÓN PHOTOGRAPHY, Minneapolis, Minnesota
p. 9, Capitol entrance; **p. 44,** Capitol rotunda; **p. 49,** marble columns; **p. 50,** *L'Etoile du Nord* ceiling decoration by Elmer Garnsey; **p. 51,** ironwork gophers; **p. 52,** *Winnowing*, lunette by Elmer Garnsey, 1905, and lady's slipper capitals; **p. 54,** *The Contemplative Spirit of the East*, mural by Kenyon Cox, ca. 1905; **p. 56–57,** *The Civilization of the Northwest*, murals by Edward H. Simmons, ca. 1905; **p. 59,** *Minnesota—Granary of the World* and *The Discoverers and Civilizers Led to the Source of the Mississippi*, lunettes by Edwin Blashfield, ca. 1905; **p. 61,** *The Progress of the State*, quadriga by Daniel Chester French and Edward C. Potter, ca. 1906; **p. 68,** battle flags in rotunda; **p. 69,** Colvill statue by Catherine Backus; **p. 93,** Governor John Johnson, statue by Andrew O'Connor, 1912; **p. 95,** rathskeller eagle; **p. 97,** restored Rathskeller Café; **p. 101,** Peace Officers Memorial by Fred Richter, 1995; **p. 103,** Governor Knute Nelson Memorial by John K. Daniels, 1928; **p. 104,** *With Ethnic Pride*, statue by Carlo Brioschi, 1931; **p. 105,** House of Representatives and *Minnesota, Spirit of Government*, mural and sculpture by Carlo and Amerigo Brioschi, ca. 1938; **p. 107,** Leif Erikson, statue by John K. Daniels, 1949; **p. 109,** *Earthbound* by John K. Daniels, 1956; **p. 110,** *Lakefront DMZ*, Minnesota Vietnam Veterans Memorial by Nina Akerberg, Jake Castillo, Rick Laffin, and Stanton Sears, 1982; **p. 111,** Minnesota Korean War Memorial by Art Norby, Bob Kost, and Dean Olson, 1998; **p. 112,** Roy Wilkins Memorial by Curtis Patterson, 1995; **p. 113,** *The Boy and the Man*, Charles Lindbergh statue by Paul Granlund, 1985.

LEIGH ROETHKE COLLECTION
p. 32, U.S. Capitol, postcard, ca. 1930s; **p. 33,** Iowa State Capitol, postcard, ca. 1910; **p. 42,** Woolworth Building, postcard, 1910.

LIBRARY OF CONGRESS, Washington, D.C.
p. 62, Daniel Chester French in studio.

MINNESOTA HISTORICAL SOCIETY, St. Paul, Minnesota
p. 2, stone columns, photograph, ca. 1899; **p. 4,** *View of St. Paul (Wabasha Streetscape)*, oil by Nicholas Richard Brewer, ca. 1908; **p. 13,** postcard, ca. 1910; **p. 14,** breaking ground, photograph by Dickey and Strong, 1896; **p. 16,** *The Signing of the Treaty of Traverse des Sioux*, oil painting by Francis Davis Millet, ca. 1905; **p. 17,** *St. Paul*, oil painting by S. Holmes Andrews, 1855; **p. 18,** *Minnesota Harvest Field*, oil painting by Joseph Rusling Meeker, 1877; **p. 19,** Central House, ca. 1850; **p. 20,** *Van Dusen Elevator*, oil on canvas by Alexis Jean Fournier, 1888; **p. 21,** Minnesota's first Capitol, photograph by Whitney's Gallery, ca. 1853; **p. 25,** Chapel of St. Paul, oil painting by John Schmitt, 1845; **p. 26,** "Jolly Joe" Rolette, pastel, artist unknown, ca. 1900; **p. 28,** laying the cornerstone, photograph by Haas Brothers, July 27, 1898; **p. 30,** State Capitol, postcard from drawing by Cass Gilbert, 1898; **p. 36,** carving stone eagles, ca. 1901; **p. 39,** Minnesota's Capitol in butter, 1901 Pan-American Exposition, 1901; **p. 40,** Minnesota's Capitol in cake, 1985; **p. 41,** Cass Gilbert, photograph by Pach, 1907; **p. 43,** Cass Gilbert and staff of Capitol architects; **p. 46,** St. Paul panorama, souvenir postcard of photograph by Francis L. Wright, 1904; **p. 47,** Capitol Room restaurant, photograph by Kenneth M. Wright Studios, ca. 1950s; Capitol souvenir pillow cover, 1915; Minnesota centennial parade float, 1958; **p. 54,** restoring *The Contemplative Spirit of the East*, photograph by Elizabeth M. Hall, 1979; **p. 63,** Le Nord cigar label, ca. 1906; **p. 64,** living flag, 1905; **p. 66,** transferring battle flags to new Capitol, June 14, 1905; **p. 67,** *U.S.S. Minnesota* float, Flag Day parade, 1905; **p. 70,** Governor Theodore Christianson and Alexander Ramsey descendants dedicate plaque, 1929; **p. 72,** Governor's Reception Room, postcard on paper, V. O. Hammon Publishing Company, ca. 1906; **p. 73,** *The Battle of Gettysburg*, oil painting by Rufus Zogbaum; **p. 74,** *The Battle of Nashville*, painting by Howard Pyle; **p. 76,** *Father Hennepin at the Falls of St. Anthony*, oil painting by Douglas Volk, ca. 1905; **p. 78,** legislators in Senate Chamber, 1905; **p. 80,** flag of the Twenty-Eighth Virginia, oil on canvas by John A. Weide, 1895; **p. 82,** Governor John Johnson, wife Elinore, dog Ray, ca. 1905; **p. 84,** naturalization ceremony, photograph by Eugene D. Becker, 1976; **p. 86,** St. Paul Winter Carnival festivities, photograph by Randolph Studio, 1917; **p. 87,** Minnesota Twins' World Series parade, 1991, 1970; **p. 88,** farmers bring cow and horse to Capitol, photograph by *St. Paul Daily News*, 1935; **p. 89,** Eisenhower campaign blimp, photograph by *St. Paul Dispatch-Pioneer Press*, 1952; **p. 90,** Hubert H. "Skip" Humphrey III with Girl Scouts, ca. 1990; **p. 91,** Governor Rudy G. Perpich and Lola Perpich, oil by Mark Balma, 2000, and Governor Floyd B. Olson, oil on canvas by Carl Bohnen, 1937; **p. 92,** Governor Arne Carlson, oil on canvas by Stephen Gjertson, 1999; **p. 93,** Governor John Johnson memorial cigars, 1910; **p. 98,** Cathedral of St. Paul, drawing by Emmanuel L. Masqueray, in *The Western Architect*, October 1908; **p. 99,** Archbishop John Ireland, pastel on paper, artist unknown, ca. 1910; **p. 100,** Capitol approach area, photograph by Marv Kruskopf, ca. 1954; **p. 102,** dedication of Governor Johnson statue, 1912; **p. 108,** John K. Daniels with model of Leif Erikson statue, 1949.

N. D. THOMPSON PUBLISHING COMPANY, St. Louis, Missouri
Dream City, Halsey C. Ives, 1893: **p. 35,** Court of Honor, World's Columbian Exposition; **p. 62,** Columbus quadriga, World's Columbian Exposition, by Daniel Chester French and Edward C. Potter, 1893.

PIONEER PRESS COMPANY, St. Paul, Minnesota
"The Bread and Butter State." Report of the Minnesota Board of Managers for the 1901 Pan-American Exposition at Buffalo, New York, 1902: **p. 38,** Fort Snelling in apples.

STAR TRIBUNE, Minneapolis, Minnesota
p. 94, Elmer Andersen lying in state, 2004; **p. 96,** restoring rathskeller murals, 1999.

STEPHEN OSMAN COLLECTION
p. 81, Marshall Sherman, photograph by Joel Emmmons Whitney, ca. 1864.

THOMAS BLANCK COLLECTION
p. 22, Minnesota's second State Capitol, lithograph by Pioneer Press Company, St. Paul, Minnesota; and *The Capitol of Minnesota* (see B. F. Forster).

INDEX

INDEX

Minnesota's Capitol: A Centennial Story
Designed by Mary Susan Oleson
Nashville, Tennessee

Composed in
Baskerville, Onyx, and Rage Italic